SILENT VICTIMS, DOMESTIC VIOLENCE DOES NOT DISCRIMINATE

HOW I TRANSCENDED FROM BEING SUBJECTED TO VARIOUS FORMS OF ABUSE, TO BECOMING WHO I AM TODAY, BLESSED AND VICTORIOUS

I0167164

YOLANDA JONES

Domestic Violence, Inc.

Contents

Acknowledgments i

Preface iii

1: Physical Abuse 1

2: Verbal Abuse 52

3: Psychological Abuse 69

4: Spousal Sexual Abuse 73

Recap 77

Signs That You May Be in a Domestic Violence Relationship 81

Signs That You Are a Victim in a Domestic Violence Cycle of Abuse 85

Helpful Tips for Loving and Pampering Me 87

Who Am I Today? 89

Acknowledgments

I would like to thank all my prayer warriors for their ongoing prayers, support and spiritual encouragements.

Special thanks to all my true Brooklynese Supporters, who do not allow themselves to conform with the majority, but know how to stay true to themselves, by never forgetting where they came from.

Special thanks to a very special person who assisted me in brainstorming for just the right title for this book, and editing. You know who you are.

Special thanks to my family for their never ending support, with regards to respecting my free expression, creativity and their unconditional love.

Special thanks to my two beautiful adult children. It is a true honor to be your mother; we have been through a lot together. I am very proud of you.

Special thanks to my father for assisting with organizing the perfect biography photo for this book.

Special thanks to my BFF (Best Female Friend) and sister of thirty-nine years. Thank you for ongoing years of loyalty.

Special thanks to my Battle-Buddy for your unwavering support and unconditional love; most of all, thank you for always having my back.

Last, and certainly not least, I Thank the Lord for he is not through with me yet!!!!!!

Preface

Domestic Violence is a very serious problem in today's society, more now than ever. It has become more prevalent especially involving our professional athletes, military families, high school and college students. There are many questions surrounding why an individual remain in an abusive relationship. Oftentimes the individual remains in the abusive relationship, because of the fear of losing their children or financial reasons.

When a battered woman separate from her husband, boyfriend, or significant other, she fears the risks of losing her children if she lacks the funds to support them on her own. Many women leave abusive relationships when they begin to see the detrimental effects of domestic violence on their children. Yet, sometimes the effects of domestic violence are difficult to see if the children are not being physically abused themselves.

During the abuse, the children feel confused, guilty, sad and angry that they are not able to protect their mother, or that they are the cause of the problem. If she leaves, the children may feel responsible for the family breakup. The children who witness their mother being abused will often suffer from physiological symptoms. Some of the physiological symptoms that the children will experience are, bed wetting, eating disorder, stomach ulcers, worrying, depression, withdrawal and preventing themselves from getting close or trusting other people, and high level of anxiety.

Some women may endure their own abuse, believing it is more important for the family to stay together, while not realizing how the abuse is affecting the children.

Believe it or not, many abusive fathers have sought and been awarded custody of their children after the divorce has been finalized. However, a number of states have passed laws that require judges to consider evidence of spouse abuse in child custody determinations.

In order to mend a healthy society of individuals whom either was subjected to or witnessed domestic violence as children, we must be able to help them move pass this cycle of abuse by educating society as a whole; so that, this epidemic does not continue to plague are future generations.

I pray that this book will Inspire, Encourage, Empower and be a Blessing to all those who read it, as it has for me

GOD BLESS!!!!

1

Physical Abuse

Physical abuse is defined as the use of physical force that may result in bodily injury, physical pain, or impairment. Physical abuse may include but is not limited to such acts of violence as striking (with or without an object), hitting, beating, pushing, shoving, shaking, slapping, kicking, pinching, and burning.

—Wikipedia: The Free Encyclopedia, 2015

Yes, I've been hit, beaten, choked, dragged, and punched. As I shared in my first book, *Scarred, but not Broken*, I experienced physical abuse; I felt it, I lived it, and I tolerated it. I remember it all from the very beginning to the very end. No one ever knew because sharing something so inhumane was, in my mind, too embarrassing to tell my family or even my closest friend. Besides, I was the second oldest, and I was supposed to set an example for my younger siblings.

It was around late spring, and I was a freshman at a local junior college. Just like any eighteen- or nineteen-year-old, I had dreams. I had many dreams. One of my dreams was to be a model—yes, a runaway model or even a commercial model.

My parents had even enrolled me in a local modeling school so I could learn the basics of modeling. I can't recall the name of the modeling agency because that was over thirty years ago. However, I do remember being taught how to apply makeup appropriately, without caking it like many women do today. I also remember being taught the difference between night and day makeup, as well as what colors accentuated a woman's eyes, nose, cheeks, and lips. Most importantly, I was taught that makeup is exactly that: "make up." Meaning that makeup is used to enhance what is already there, not cover up what God has blessed us women with.

Another dream of mine was to attend law school and pursue a law degree. Well, I completed my undergraduate studies in criminal justice by receiving an associate and a bachelor's degree. I was so close, yet so far away, to sitting for the LSAT (Law School Admission Test), and depending on my LSAT score, I could have begun to apply to some law schools. Nevertheless, life choices happened and gave me a new perspective or, should I say, outlook on the direction I wanted to go.

I digress. There will be more about my life's decisions throughout the book.

How I met my children's father was so like a fairy tale. While walking down the stairs to my next class in the basement (lower level) of the classroom building I ran into him. He was mopping the stairwell's floors, and I remember him saying to me, "Oh my God, heaven is missing an angel." Yes, he was a janitor, and I did not turn my nose up at him; neither did I mistreat or judge him just because of his job title.

Growing up as a young girl, I was taught not to judge someone just because of the type of work he or she did. I had always been taught to treat people with respect.

I was young and giddy, so I blushed when I heard his comment. I remember exactly what I wore that day: it was white, all white. I wore a pair of white Lee jeans; a short-sleeve, button-down, white ruffled blouse; white open-toe pumps; and some white clips in my hair. Huh, back then I wore a beginning stage of jheri curls. Yes, back in the eighties, jheri curls were the *shiznick*.

Although I found his comment appealing, I also found him to be attractive, even more so. He was well built, with a bright complexion, long jheri curls, and a well-defined mustache. For some reason, during my growing and immature years, I had a fascination with lighter skinned males—no reason, I just found them attractive.

He had a muscular physique as though he worked out daily. You could tell that he took time to iron his uniform because it looked crisp and neat. He was all put together, not a wrinkle anywhere. Most importantly, he always smelled good; he either wore Brut 33 or Old Spice. Today, I hate the smell of either one. For starters, I associate these smells with what I was subjected to by his hands; secondly, these smells simply turn my stomach.

Well, every day from that point on, he and I continued to cross paths. There was never a day that went by without us seeing each other. To this day, I believe he took the time to learn my class schedule; he knew when I was arriving at school and when I was leaving. He even knew what days, what time, and where I had dance and cheerleader practice after school.

Back then I was gullible, naive; I simply thought it was fate or just coincidental. But now, since many years have gone by, I've had time to process what transpired and how I came to be subjected to the man who once said he "loved me" and became the father of my now two adult children. It is clear that he, like many predators, was on the prowl. He saw my innocence; he saw my vulnerability.

Our first date was at Grandy's Restaurant, and I remember this day as though it was yesterday. I ordered a chicken-fried steak, baked beans, green beans, a dinner roll, sweet iced tea, and a cinnamon roll for dessert. He was such a gentleman, or so I thought. Anytime we went anywhere, he would open the door to the car, store, or restaurant. I thought I had my prince. I believed I was grown. That's right, it was what my mind wanted me to believe.

But I was not mentally grown in the sense of being mentally mature, nor was I ready for what lay ahead for me.

I recall being excited and sharing with our local church bishop that I was engaged and that I was going to get married. I will never forget what my bishop asked me: "Is he saved?" My response was "Well, he knows the Lord." My bishop asked again as though I was not listening, "Is he saved?" At this point, and because I had allowed myself to get caught up in the moment of being "grown," I didn't care if he was or was not saved. I was just happy that I was dating someone older than me, who has been in the service and had life experience.

At this point, since I was not able to lie to my bishop, he already knew. My bishop shared, "If he is not saved, don't marry him because you will be unequally yoked." Wow, at that moment, I was no longer happy. My spirit felt conflicted, yet I ignored all advice and future signs. This would become one of the first signs that I should have taken heed to, but I didn't.

But it shall come to pass, if thou wilt not hearken unto the voice of the Lord, thy God, to observe to do all his commandments and his statutes which I command this day; that all these curse shall come upon thee, and overtake thee (Deuteronomy 28:15).

After all, he had been in the army but was no longer on active duty. I don't recall the exact number of years he served; however, I do know that when I met him, he was an army reservist attached to a local communication unit in the Dallas/Seagoville area. I had no knowledge of, and will never know, why he was separated from active duty or discontinued his status in the US Army Reserve. I only know what he shared with me. According to him, he did not like having to "kiss anyone's ass."

Hmm, imagine that. This appeared to be the same reason and behavioral patterns he encountered on all his civilian jobs after that.

Fast forward to a year later. We were six months into our marriage with our son. Yes, our son was nine months old, and my husband's true nature was beginning to reveal itself more and more every day. He had also become very confrontational at home and at work. It was as though I was now married to night and day. Some days he was thoughtful, respectful, and lovable—a gentleman. Other times I hated and despised him. Many days I regretted being married, yet I wanted my marriage to work.

I was raised by my paternal grandparents who taught me to stand by and support my husband, no matter what challenges we were experiencing. Besides, I had confidence in him and in our marriage. Or could it be that I was just living in a fantasy world of what I dreamed my first marriage should have been?

Confidence in an unfaithful man in time of trouble is like a broken tooth, and a foot out of joint (Proverbs 25:19).

The majority of our arguing revolved around finances—never having enough money and never knowing where it was going—considering that we both were working, and between the two of us, we had four jobs. Other times our arguing was because of his drinking or his family's interference and negative influences in our marriage. Yes, his drinking went from drinking a can or two after work, to drinking a forty-ounce along with one to two cans of beer after work, to drinking a can of beer while he, as he used to say, "sh-showered-shaved."

At this point, I knew there was a problem. When I would address my concerns regarding his overindulging in alcohol, especially in the mornings before going to work, he always denied that he had a drinking problem, along with becoming agitated that I even brought it up. His drinking began to spill over into his workplace. His supervisor would even telephone me to inform me that my husband had reported to work with alcohol on his breath and was easily agitated, arguing and cursing the supervisor.

Wow, seriously? Who does that? Yes, some days he was a functioning alcoholic, and other days he was a belligerent alcoholic.

I couldn't believe what I was hearing. His supervisor actually was asking for my assistance. He wanted me to talk to my husband about his drinking as if he (the supervisor) had become afraid and intimidated by his own employee. His supervisor shared with me that if I didn't talk to my husband, he would be on the verge of being terminated from his position.

It was evident that his supervisor was trying to take some positive measures to intervene by reaching out to me for my help, so my husband would not be terminated. Despite his alcohol use, my husband was well known at work, as well as being very dependable and a hard worker. But his excessive alcohol use continued, and he continued to have issues at work with his supervisor and coworkers.

He was no longer dependable, and his coworkers no longer had anything nice to say about him. He was no longer likable at home or at work.

Because I grew up in an alcoholic environment with my paternal family, I knew the signs of an alcoholic. I saw the signs; I felt and lived them. I knew I was married and living with an alcoholic, but he was in denial. The more I addressed my concerns regarding the extent of his excessive drinking, the more he denied that he had a problem.

Wine is a mocker, strong drink is raging; and whosoever is deceived thereby is not wise (Proverbs 20:1).

His excessive alcohol intake became so uncontrollable that he didn't care what he did, what he said, or who he hurt. He became numb. He no longer was the man I met a year ago in the college stairwell. He was no longer the man who showered me with his politeness and gentlemanly persona. He was no longer the man I fell in love with; he had become a stranger to me. I no longer knew who he was. It felt strange living under the same roof with him.

One Friday evening, he agreed to go to the store to buy the baby some milk, baby food, and Pampers since he had been home the majority of the evening and I had just arrived home from choir practice.

However, I have no idea where he went, but I do know he left at about six thirty and did not return until close to midnight. I was very disappointed in him, let alone upset, because the baby was hungry, and I was out of Pampers (although I improvised by feeding the baby some mashed potatoes and wrapping him in a cloth diaper).

When I asked where he had been, by the time I realized he had been drinking, it was too late. He dropped the bags, threw me down on the living room couch, straddled me, and began choking me. You would have thought I was a burglar who broke into his home because he choked me so hard that I began to see silver specs floating in my eyes, not knowing I was losing oxygen to my brain. Yes, he was slowing killing me, and I was dying.

For the drunkard and the glutton shall come to poverty: and drowsiness shall clothe a man with rags (Proverbs 23:21).

I never shared this incident with my parents or other maternal relatives, especially not my cousins (I have close to one hundred first, second, and third cousins). I definitely was not going to tell any of my male cousins because I come from a family of strong bonds, in which an eye for an eye is an understatement.

Most importantly, I was ashamed but mostly shocked that this man whom I married would or could do something so violent. Sharing with my family what happened, or even getting an annulment, would appear as though I had given up on my marriage; and giving up on my marriage, or not being supportive by getting help for my husband, was unthinkable.

Truthfully, I didn't believe I would financially survive being a single parent. I didn't want to succumb to being a single mom statistic, nor did I want to move with my son back into my parents' home. No, I had too much pride. Yes, my pride would not have allowed that.

Pride goeth before destruction, and a haughty spirit before a fall (Proverbs 16:18).

As I mentioned in my first book, *Scarred, but not Broken*, Therefore, I was willing to do just that. I didn't know any other way; after all, I was grown, playing house, and believing that if I stayed with him, I could *change* him. Yes, I actually believed that people could change people.

And yes, I was immature to think like this because only God can change people's hearts; people cannot change people. This was something I had to learn, and I learned it the hard way.

During the time he was choking me, I was praying, "God help me; don't let this man kill me." All of a sudden, he let go and walked away as if nothing happened. That night I was afraid to sleep, not knowing if I was going to awaken in the middle of the night with this man's hands around my neck again. So I didn't sleep too well. As a matter of fact, I slept with one eye open and the other closed. It was a long night, and I was sleepy and had to go to work the next morning, but I was afraid to sleep.

Peace I leave with you, my peace I give unto you: not as the world giveth, give I unto you. Let not your heart be troubled, neither let it be afraid (John 14:27).

The thought of my husband choking me just wouldn't leave my mind; I was still in shock that he could do such a thing. If anyone had ever told me that there was going to come a day when my husband would almost choke me to death, I would not have believed it. But he did, and I continued to stay with him, thinking he would not do it again. After all, he apologized the next morning, stating that he didn't know what came over him. He assured me that he wouldn't do it again.

Days later, I guess his conscience got the best of him because, out of the blue, he stated that he had never hit or put his hands on a woman before. Really? I wasn't convinced. This was hard to believe because, at the time he was choking me, it appeared that he was familiar with that behavior and his actions were nothing new, even to him. No, he appeared all too sure of himself, as if he knew that choking me would give him satisfaction and the perfect "Stanford" wife.

I once heard a famous, powerful African American female comedian say, "Wouldn't it be nice if men came with a warning label?" Yes, my sentiment exactly. It would be great if *people* came with a warning la-bel, not just men, because I'm certain there are many men who feel the same way about the psycho women with whom they involve them-selves with. So, just like there are psycho and abusive men out there, the same is true for unbalanced women.

Wow, just think of being forewarned about the person you allow your-self to get involved with. Wouldn't it be a great thing to read on his or her label: "Beware, this person will one day choke you and almost kill you, and has a history of alcohol and drug problems," or "Beware, this woman will use your children to get to you," or "Beware, one day this man will run off with your children," or "Beware, this man or woman is going to cheat on you," or "Beware, this man or woman will steal from you," or "Beware, this person is going to run up your credit cards."

Knowledge is power and is a beautiful thing

Here's an even better one that I'm certain many are familiar with: "Beware, this man or woman is going to play you like a fiddle." Even though this person has no desire to marry you, instead being man or women enough to tell you so, he or she goes along playing with your heart and emotions. No, this type of individual would rather just milk the cow and get the milk for free instead of buying the entire cow. Why should they? They're getting the milk for free, and they know it.

Yes, being forewarned of the type of man or woman we allow ourselves to get involved with would be a beautiful thing. But then again, we would be living in a perfect world, and no one is without spot or wrinkle, although there are many who think they are flawless, especially those whom we come in contact with on a day-to-day basis.

Be ye therefore perfect, even as your father which is in heaven is perfect (Matthew 6:48).

I know one thing: it sure as heck would alleviate wasting your time on a person who does not have your best interest at heart. Too often we women, and men, waste our precious time on individuals who don't appreciate us, let alone deserve us (good thing), respect us, or treat us like the queen and king that we are.

A good man obtaineth favour of the Lord: but a man of wicked devices will be condemn. A man shall not be established by wickedness: but the root of the righteous shall not be moved. A virtuous woman is a crown to her husband: but she that maketh ashamed is as rottenness in his bones (Proverbs 12:2–4).

Who can find a virtuous woman? For her price is far above rubies (Proverbs 31:10).

Because I was still in a state of shock, my mind, body, and spirit was at unrest. I couldn't sleep, eat, or think. Part of my mind was telling me that what he had done was not right and I needed to leave him, yet another part of my brain was telling me that he didn't mean it and he loved me, and had I not upset him, he wouldn't have done what he did.

I now had fallen in a deep depression and was feeling down from the time I woke up through the majority of the day. I found myself either sleeping too much or not feeling as though I had gotten enough sleep. It appeared that my natural energy had been sucked out of me, and I had begun losing a lot of weight. Sadly, I no longer was interested in my church activities of singing in the choir and participating in the prison ministry, let alone being interested in any church events. I began to have difficulty making decisions or even concentrating day to day at work.

I had even started to blame myself and lose all self-worth. The more I listened to my mind, the more I felt guilty, that it was my fault, when in actuality it was not me but him who needed help. I just happened to be in his path and at the wrong time.

Over the years I've learned that people who struggle with alcohol addiction know exactly what they are doing; the alcohol just numbs them from feeling. In other words, when they are in an alcohol-induced state, they don't care about the consequences of their actions or behavior. It's as if the alcohol is their liquid courage to do and say whatever they want, and that's exactly what they do.

After a few months had gone by, I was still in my deep depression and began to worry about what-ifs. I was worrying about things that had not happened, but I knew that they could happen. I was afraid of the unknown. So I telephoned my aunt (God rest her soul) and asked if I could stay with her for a while. And I did.

Yes, I had became a worrier by creating my own collection of worst-case scenarios and images that could possibly happen, instead of staying and confronting my fears. I had become heavily guarded for the what- ifs that could happen. Not only did I lose my self-worth during this ordeal, but I'd also lost my self-esteem.

As I began to plan for my travel to visit with my aunt and uncle, I knew my visit would be short, considering that my aunt and uncle resided in army base housing. However, I just needed time away from my husband in order to process all that had happened and the steps I needed to take for an annulment. Most importantly, I now had to think about my son and the life we would have: a single mother without any advanced education other than a high school diploma, and a son growing up without his father active in his life.

While staying with my aunt and uncle, and due to the stressors of my marriage and severity of my depression, I had a mild stroke while watching television in the living room with my cousin. I remember it as though it was yesterday. First my eyesight went blurry and I saw floaters in my eyes. Then my tongue became heavy, that I was not able to form a complete word or sentence, and my right arm felt so heavy that I was not able to raise it. My entire right side (arms, hands, face) had gone completely numb.

During this state of numbness, I began to think if my husband's choking didn't kill me, then something internal was about to kill me.

My aunt and uncle rushed me to the base hospital, but since I was visiting and not a dependent, the doctors were reluctant to tend to me. However, because my uncle was well known on base, the doctors made an exception and examined me. I was told that I would need to follow up with my private physician upon my return to Texas, which I did. And although I did not want to return to Texas—or to my abusive husband—I knew I had to return to see my private medical provider.

After spending two weeks with my aunt and uncle, I returned to Texas and immediately made an appointment with my primary care provider. The news I received was bittersweet. My doctor informed me that I was pregnant with my second child. I immediately cried because my plan was to file for an annulment and move back to Brooklyn, New York, to raise my son with the help, support, and protection of my maternal family, with all my maternal cousins showering me with their love.

Returning to New York would have been my safe haven; I knew if I had returned to New York, I would be well protected by my uncles and male cousins. Most importantly, my son would have been surrounded by strong, educated African American males, who would be great role models for him. Instead, I stayed in Texas.

Yes, I remained with my husband because I didn't want my children being raised by another man, who would not be their biological father, and I didn't want to remarry and have more children. No, I did not want a blended family; instead I wanted to give everything I had to repair what was broken in my marriage.

I still wanted the fairy tale, the white-picket-fence type of marriage. So I stayed.

Things were great for the next year and a half—no arguing, perfect harmony, and fun times during the holidays, birthdays, and our first anniversary. I thought the nightmares were over. He had even stopped drinking as much as he had before and had begun accompanying the children and me to church.

Our finances had even started to improve. In addition, he had begun preparing breakfast on the weekends and dinners when he arrived home early from work; he'd even assist in dropping off and picking up the children from day care. He'd become so helpful around the home, more so than ever. His conversations with me regarding our family's future were positive, and he was pursuing his GED. Things were looking great for our family and us.

But it didn't last long.

Apparently, my encounter with abuse at the hands of my husband had just begun, but at that time, I was not educated about the cycle of domestic violence, particularly regarding the "honeymoon" phase. I later learned of these phases while pursuing my undergraduate and graduate degrees.

Domestic violence is nothing new but has been going on for centuries. As the title of this book states, domestic violence does not discriminate. There isn't any nationality, culture, or socioeconomic status exempt from domestic violence.

As a matter of fact, some cultures actually condone domestic violence. Many do not label abuse against the spouse as "domestic violence," and there are still some cultures that see women as property. Nevertheless, although the time and faces of the perpetrators or abusers change, their tactics and the phases of domestic violence remain the same.

I had no idea that, up to this point, I had already been subjected to three of the four phases of domestic violence during the first four years of my marriage. Yes, I had already gone through phases one through three:

- **Phase One:** Our constant verbal arguments over the finances and in-laws. This phase is known as the **Tension** phase.

- **Phase Two:** The actual abuse, the choking incident. This phase is known as the **Acting Out, Abusive** phase.

- **Phase Three:** My husband feeling guilty of his abuse, expressing his remorse, being apologetic, and stating that he would never do it again. This phase is known as the **Reconciliation, Guilty** phase.

While enjoying the temporary peace in our home (and if my recollections are vivid), I remember a gentleman, a new friend of my husband, who began making frequent visits to our home. There was something uncomfortable about this man's energy. It was evil; it was as if my spirit knew who this man was, who allowed himself to befriend my husband and often invite himself to our home. Yes, it was the master manipulator himself in the image of man. I didn't know at that moment, but I began to put two and two together.

Every time there was harmony in my home and between my husband and me, this man would make himself present. I observed the secrecy he and my husband shared each time he came around to visit. He and my husband would go to the bedroom and close the door, or they would step out and go for a ride.

I was naive and didn't think anything of it. After all, my marriage was still in harmony. I was at peace, my home was peaceful, and I was a young mom and still clueless.

The thief cometh not, but for to steal and to kill, and to destroy: I am come that they might have life, and that they might have it more abundantly (John 10:10).

It finally came to me a year later when I gave birth to our daughter, who fought her way into life. Yes, she was a blessing from God. Although I carried her for one month over my due date, her lungs were not fully developed and she had to receive a blood transfusion.

It was at this time that my husband confessed that he had been using drugs (cocaine) and the person who was visiting our home was his drug dealer. Wow, my uneasy feelings regarding this man were right on point. My discernment was correct.

My spirit knew that this man was not good for my family, let alone good company for my husband. I became angry because, unbeknownst to me, my daughter had been conceived with sperm infected by drugs and could have died. Thus, I began questioning my husband's morality.

How could a parent jeopardize the innocent life of his or her unborn? Not only was it selfish but it also was careless.

As I mentioned in my first book, another incident occurred. My husband had been placed on medical leave, due to a head-on collision with another 18-wheeler, at which time he relocated us to Illinois. Still a young mother and wife, I thought everything was still going to be fine, as long as our family remained together.

I didn't have any reservations about leaving, since there hadn't been any more outbursts or physical encounters by him in the past year and that unidentified man was not visiting our home anymore, prior to us leaving Texas. However, relocating to Illinois was not a good move, and that is expressing my reservations mildly, very mildly.

For starters, we were deceived about a home that we were to move into. I won't go in to long details; let's just say this home was not fit for an animal to live in. It did not have working electricity or plumbing, or a roof. As a matter of fact, the plumbing (toilet) was not in place; you could see the hole in the floor. Oh yes, you read that right. It did not have a roof, which allowed any and everything from nature to either fly or crawl inside.

The lip of truth shall be established for ever: but a lying tongue is but for a moment (Proverbs 12:19).

You might as well say we were homeless, because this place was not fit for living.

This place was not fit to live in, and we were not going to move our furniture into it right away either. I can't recall the particulars of where we stored our furniture, but I do remember that we had to place many mouse and rat sticky traps everywhere, so we wouldn't be bitten during the night. Sleeping on the floor on top of blankets was no picnic.

Yes, these were the conditions we were subjected to, and I was far away from my family, and I had resigned from a good-paying job with benefits.

Nights in this place were never-ending and frightening. Hearing the constant noise and clattering across the room from what we suspected were mice and other critters were alarming. I recall awakening one morning to check the sticky traps, only to notice that the trap had caught a baby bird that had flown in through the open roof.

Thank God it never rained the first week. Who knows what would have transpired, let alone what could have happened to my then five-year-old son and 1½-year-old baby girl, from being subjected to these inhumane conditions.

On another morning I woke up to discover that the sticky trap had this time caught a recluse spider. Yes, a recluse, one of the most deadly spiders known to mankind. Catching a recluse spider in the sticky trap was the straw that broke the camel's back, and we moved out of the place until the building and remodeling were complete.

Yes, we moved out of that shack. Yes, I said shack because that's exactly what it was…a shack, a barn, whatever ungodly name you'd call a place that's unfit for a human to live in.

Until the shack was repaired, we moved in with my in-laws. Let's just say it felt as if someone had poured salt on an open wound of mine. Residing with my in-laws resulted in another battle and hurdle I had to fight and overcome, day in and day out. Every day I felt as if I was in a *Twilight* movie. I knew I did not belong, especially not there. I had no family in Illinois, and all of his relatives were either in the surrounding Illinois cities or Chicago.

Although we were married, I felt lost, and it was at this time that I discovered we had nothing in common. We were so different, from our like and dislikes to how we were raised, from our religion and spiritual beliefs to our goals for life and educational goals, from how we wanted to raise our children to the boundaries of our families. A realization hit me at that moment that I actually did not know this man. I knew he was my husband and I'd had two of his children, but I never allowed myself to get to know him. To add insult to injury, this was only my second time meeting his family.

Another realization hit me that I had married a total stranger. I knew nothing about him, his family, or his family background—nothing. Yes, I knew his Social Security number, his date of birth, and the date we got married, but that wasn't enough. I began to ask myself, "What did I get myself into?"

Marriage is supposed to be a beautiful thing, but there was more about him and his family and the secrets within that I did not know. Honestly, I didn't care; I just wanted my in-laws to do their thing and leave me and my husband and children alone to do ours, to be a family without their negative influences.

For I would that all men were even as I myself. But every man hath his proper gift of God, one after this manner, and another after that. I say therefore to the unmarried and widows, It is good for them if they abide even as I. But if they cannot contain, let them marry; for it is better to marry than to burn (1 Corinthians 7:7–9).

Nevertheless, throughout the entire time we lived with his family, I did not believe I was married because oftentimes my place as a wife was overridden by my mother-n-law. She was the matriarch of his family and ran everything and everyone in and out of her home. Never did he stand up to protect me against his mother.

Therefore shall a man leave his father and his mother, and shall cleave unto his wife; and they shall be one flesh (Genesis 2:24).

As I recall, less than a month after we moved in with his family, he resumed working with the over-the-road truck company, so he was gone often for months at a time, leaving us with his family. On one evening, while the children were asleep, his mother and I got into a verbal altercation. She said that, although she loved her grandchildren, she did not like me and wished her son had not chosen to marry me, and that I was not good enough for him.

I could not believe my ears. The first thing that went through my mind was what have I done or didn't do to this woman that she had such a distaste for me when she didn't even know me?

As a matter of fact, she and I did not meet one another until after her son and I had said our "I dos," and this was our second introduction. So what was the real underlying issue, and why was she projecting it on me?

Believe it or not, she is not the first nor will she be the last mother-in-law to express her distaste for her daughter-in-law. I'm sure there are millions of mothers-in-law who would like to have their sons marry the woman they choose. Unfortunately, it is very sad that these mothers-in-law have boundary issues and simply do not know their place after their sons have taken a wife.

Ironically, this is another form of domestic violence because it involves power and control of a family member; this just happened to be my husband's mother, a woman whom he held dear in his heart. Now he was placed in a battle between his wife and his mother who conceived him.

Nevertheless, we went back and forth, and because of my strong personality, I was not easily broken or turned into a puppet. This did not go over well with her. Instead this pissed her off even more since she could not easily control me. And as a result, in the heat of our altercation, she raised her hand to take a hit at me. However, her attempt was unsuccessful because I blocked her strike, which caused her to fall back against the sink.

She lied once again to my husband, saying that I pushed her, and to my surprise he as well as others in his family believed every word. It was evident that there was a serious case of over-enmeshment boundary issues—no one was allowed to deviate from what was believed to be the family norms.

No weapon that is formed against thee shall prosper; and every tongue that shall rise against thee in judgment thou shalt condemn. This is the heritage of the servants of the Lord, and their righteousness is of me, saith the Lord (Isaiah 54:17).

There were other things that happened involving many of his family members that tainted and poisoned our marriage; but either he was blind, or he simply just ignored addressing the issues. Whatever his reasons for not coming to my aid, it caused me to become heavily guarded day in and day out. I was not able to trust him or anyone in the household, and Lord knows I was afraid to eat the foods that were often prepared.

The Lord is my rock and my fortress, and my deliverer; my God, my strength, in whom I will trust; my buckler, and the horn of my salvation, and my high tower. I will call upon the Lord, who is worthy to be praised: so shall I be saved from mine enemies (Psalm 18:2–3).

The second physical abuse from my husband occurred less than a year after relocating to Illinois. The home that we were supposed to have resided in was finally in a workable condition, and because I had the gift of taking nothing and turning it into something, I was able to do just that. Although it was not my ideal or dream home, I made the best of it with what I had.

And all things, whatsoever ye shall ask in prayer, believing, ye shall receive (Matthew 21:22).

I was able to buy material and make curtains for all the rooms. I used old rugs to design a carpet wall and designed a diamond-shaped mirror wall in my living room. I had even taken old scrap metal and turned it into artifacts for our home. It was not a rich home, nor was it worth a lot, but it was our home. And after I put my touch, love, and creativity to work, it was a home worth living in.

One afternoon I was sitting on the living room couch and studying. I had already bathed the children, fed them some ravioli, and put them in bed. The evening was quiet, and my husband was still out with his relatives. I did not worry about his whereabouts because I knew he was with family and was in Chicago.

All of a sudden, my husband arrived home with his relatives and asked why I had not cooked dinner or even made him a sandwich. Huh? As I reminisce about this incident, I can't help but think that he must have invited his relatives back to our home, expecting that I would have dinner prepared for them all. But apparently I had disappointed him and may have even made him look like a liar to his relatives.

When I told him that I had been studying, he didn't respond until after his relatives left. Then he went into the kitchen and began trying to make himself a sandwich. He asked me again, "Why didn't you cook dinner? You could have at least made me a sandwich."

My response was "I told you I have been studying, and you're in the kitchen now, so you can make yourself a sandwich." He asked, "What did you just say?" I knew by the tone and shift in his voice that he didn't like my response, so I didn't repeat myself.

All of a sudden, he rushed into the living room where I was sitting on the couch, threw my textbook out of my hand, threw all my other books onto the floor, grabbed me by my feet, and pulled me off the couch across the living room into the sunroom. He opened the front door, picked me up, and threw me out the door.

During the time he had ahold of my feet, I struggled to get his hands loose, but he grabbed tightly around my ankles. His grip was so tight, and it all happened so fast, that before I knew it I had already been picked up and thrown out the door without my blouse. Yes, my blouse had been torn off in the struggle. He didn't care that I stood outside in the cold banging on the door for him to let me in.

As I shared in my first book, I tried to gain entry into the house by banging on the door and then climbing on crates on the side of the house so I could climb through a side window. But, when he caught me trying to climb through the window, he slammed and locked it, preventing me from gaining entry. I stood there blouseless and freezing in the snow.

Meanwhile, because of our yelling and scuffling, the children woke up and began screaming and crying for him to stop and let me in. My children's pleas fell on deaf ears, and he even threatened to throw them outside with me. I felt helpless and angry, and I was afraid for my children and myself.

Once again I found myself in a dangerous situation at the hands of my husband. I had truly believed he would never put his hands on me again, but I was wrong. I guess when he put his hands on me the first time and I returned to him, it only made it easier for him to abuse me again.

And of course, I still did not share this ordeal with my family, for I was too embarrassed and fearful that they would question me about why I stayed in a marriage where I'd been abused—not once but now twice.

Abuse me once, shame on you; abuse me twice, shame on me. I was at the point of being fed up with the abuse and wanted out, but I did not know how to leave.

Growing up, I remember watching a movie about domestic violence, starring Farah Fawcett, and I remembered that she burned her abusive husband while he slept. I began to have that homicidal thought. What if I did the same? Would I be able to get away with it, or would I be tried for first-degree murder?

The more I contemplated ways of killing this man, the more I began to think of all the domestic violence shelters and resources that were now available to help women and their children. Therefore, the chances of me killing this man and not being found guilty would be slim to none. Besides, he was not worth my freedom.

And we know that all things work together for good to them that love God, to them who are called according to his purpose (Romans 8:28).

So, the next morning, after I carried out my normal day-to-day activities, I drove to a telephone booth in a nearby city, far away from my or my in-law's home. I took a more responsible and legal route: I sought help from a domestic violence hotline. I remember dialing zero for an operator because I didn't have any money. I explained to the operator that my husband had abused me and I needed help. She connected me to a local shelter.

The person on the phone immediately told me not to share too much on the phone or stay on the phone too long, because I could have been followed by my husband or he may have had someone following or watching me. Her instructions were very explicit and short.

She told me, "When it is safe" and when my husband was not at home, I should pack a suitcase for my children and me and store it in a place that he would not find it. She further instructed me not to pack all of our clothes, only enough to get us through the night and possibly the first few days.

The domestic violence staff explained it was important that he not discover my plan to leave by noticing the shortage of clothes hanging in the closet or folded in the dresser drawers. The domestic violence worker also instructed that I pack a few of my children's favorite toys but be certain not to over pack, because what we didn't have, we would receive once we were in a safe environment.

Next, I was instructed to take my children to the local police department after I picked them up from day care and school, and inform the police department that I'd been abused by my husband. Then I had to tell them that I contacted the domestic violence shelter, which instructed me to ask for police assistance to move my belongings from the house. Not once did the police officers dismiss my report, nor did I feel judged. Instead, they assisted me by assigning an officer to care for my children while two other patrol officers took me to my home to gather my suitcases that were stashed under our bed.

I followed the domestic violence instructions to a T, and sure enough, when the police escorted me back to my home to retrieve the suitcase from under the bed (which he never looked under), my husband was present. My heart felt as though it was going to jump out of my chest; I was scared and nervous. I didn't want any trouble, nor did I want anyone to be shot or killed on my account.

As one officer walked me into the house to retrieve my suitcase, another officer detained my husband outside. He was not even allowed to reach out and touch me.

For once, I actually felt safe and knew from this particular day forward, I would no longer give my husband the opportunity to harm me or threaten my children ever again.

When the officer took me back to the police station to rejoin my children, I was relieved and my children looked happy. They had no knowledge or clue of what had transpired. The police officers at the station had taken great care of my children in my brief absence. They were given ice cream and were provided coloring books and crayons. I was so appreciative of these officers for taking care of my children and saving us from any future abuse.

The officers placed the children and me in their squad car and drove us to the domestic violence shelter that was quite a ride out from the town where we lived. Within one year, my children and I were moved and placed in three domestic violence shelters in two different cities, simply to keep my husband from discovering where we were.

These officers appeared genuine and very concerned, and I was so appreciative that they respected me, but more importantly, they provided safety for my children and me. As I look back on this ordeal, I can now voice my story to help others who may be going through something similar. Some may not know how to get out, due to intense fear or other circumstances.

Oftentimes, victims may need positive guidance and an escape plan. The escape plan provided for me by the domestic violence hotline kept my children and me safe from what could had resulted in us, my husband, or the police officers being injured or killed. There have been many officers injured or killed in the line of duty, as well as innocent bystanders and family members or friends trying to come to the aid of the victim.

It is a tragedy when an abused woman and her child (or children) decide that enough is enough and try to leave, only to be faced with a roadblock by their abuser, who takes his life and theirs. In this situation, everyone loses; there are no winners. The children will never have a future, and the mother will never get a chance to see her child (or children) attend a school prom, graduate from college, marry, and have a family of his or her own.

This was my safe exit from domestic violence:

- I packed a suitcase with our clothes, just enough to get my children and me through at least three to five days (but no more than a week), because once we arrived at the safe place, we were provided more clothes and other items.

- I was certain to pack the children's favorite toys. I didn't pack too many toys, just the ones the children played with the most and that I knew they would miss if they didn't have them.

- I hid one suitcase under our bed and the other suitcase under the children's bed. I knew my husband would not look under the beds.

- I continued my daily routine; I never altered it in any way because I never wanted to let on to my husband that I was planning an escape.

- On the day of my action for a safe leave, I picked up my children from day care and school at the same time, and I took them directly to the local police department.

- I shared with the officers exactly what I was supposed to tell them, according to the instructions from the domestic violence hotline: I had been abused by my husband, and I needed a police escort to return to my home and gather our suitcases, which were stashed in a hiding place.

- I allowed an officer to stay with my children while two officers escorted me back to my home to retrieve my suitcases.

- After I retrieved my suitcases, the officers took me back to the station to be reunited with my children. Then we were taken to the undisclosed domestic violence shelter out of town. Once my children and I were in the safe environment of the shelter, the nights seemed very long for me but not for the children, for the staff welcomed us with open, loving arms.

- The first night, while the children slept peacefully, my mind wandered. How could I have allowed myself to go through this, let alone put my children through this, and end up living in a shelter?

- **At no time did I say anything evil or negative, or express any ill feelings, about their father in my children's presence. Although I actually felt hate toward their father, I shared that in confidence with my counselor and the domestic violence staff during venting and healing sessions.**

- As days went by, my children were placed in a new school, and they met new friends. Transitioning from school to school didn't appear to be difficult for them because they were young at the time, ages seven and three.

- When my children began to ask questions, my daughter would ask where her daddy was and say she wanted her daddy. I don't recall ever hearing my son ask for his father, nor do I recall him ever wanting to return to live with his father during our time at the shelter.

- My response to my little girl when she asked about her father was that we wouldn't be able to live with Daddy anymore because Daddy hurt Mommy, and Mommy was afraid that she and her brother would accidently get hurt. However, I assured her that she would have an opportunity to see her father again, but it might be a while. She never asked again about her father.

- While we resided at the shelter, there were a lot of activities provided for the children, along with the child counselors and children's event coordinators. The mothers like me often had mother time. The facilities were well organized with professional staffs. Our residency in the domestic violence shelter was in 1992–1993.

- If a man or a woman professes to love you, "Love should not hurt." Love should be expressed not so much by what is said, but more importantly, it should be expressed by genuine actions.

That was the end of being subjected to any more physical abuse at the hands of my husband or from any members from his family.

But I say unto you, Love your enemies, bless them that curse you, do good to them that hate you, and pray for them which despitefully use you, and persecute you; that ye may be the children of your Father which is in heaven: for he maketh his sun to rise on the evil and on the good, and sendeth rain on the just and on the unjust (Matthew 5:44–45).

During my domestic violence ordeal, it became difficult to trust anyone, especially since I was not from Illinois and my in-laws were well known throughout Chicago and Illinois. However, I can say that I met some awesome people that I believe God placed in my path, providing assistance, direction, and spiritual support.

For his anger endureth but a moment; in his favour is life: weeping may endure for a night, but joy cometh in the morning (Psalm 30:5).

During this time, I did not own or have access to a vehicle, and it appeared that my world had been turned upside down. Still I never wavered in my goal of pursuing my college education.

Even as a single parent, I've always resorted back to some of the positive teachings from my childhood. One important teaching that never left me, but was constantly drilled into me, was to be someone in life.

I was always told to never settle for average but always look toward perfection, advancement, and excellence in everything I did, especially when it involved education. Therefore, I continued my prelaw studies, even if it meant that I had to walk four to five miles daily to the college campus from my residence—even in three feet of snow, which resulted in me contracting pneumonia.

After leaving the domestic violence shelter, my children and I were blessed with our own home. It was nothing but the work of God because I had terrible credit, was unemployed, and could not afford a down payment for a home. However, an angel was placed in my path.

He was an older Caucasian widower who had extra property and a vacant home. His adult children, I believe, were residing in other cities throughout Illinois. Through corroborating with the domestic violence shelter, this man allowed my children and me to take occupancy in one of his homes.

Ask, and it shall be given you; seek, and ye shall find; knock, and it shall be opened unto you: for every one that asketh receiveth; and he that seeketh findeth; and to him that knocketh it shall be opened (Matthew 7:7–8).

Although my children and I were blessed with a roof over our heads, we had very little furniture, or food many nights, but we were still happy. I was at peace. I no longer had to worry about being choked, or dragged and thrown out of my home; neither did my children have to be subjected to such a violent, unstable environment. I finally found joy and peace, but that did not last too long.

To fast forward, I eventually filed for a divorce after having been physically separated for three years. When the judge asked me if there was anything I wanted, I said, "Your Honor, I want nothing from this man; all I want is the return to my maiden name." Yes, hard as it may seem to many who are reading this book, and unlike many women who try to take a man for all he has by stripping him of everything, I was different. I never was a materialistic woman and did not care for material things.

I just wanted a clean start and my freedom.

The courts, however, had other plans. They not only awarded me sole custody of our children, but I was also awarded possession of my husband's Mazda two-door pickup truck. Of course, he did not like the fact that I was awarded his truck, but the courts knew I had gone some time without a vehicle while trying to get the children and myself back and forth to school, grocery shopping, and even to the doctor's office or hospital when the children were sick.

When it rains, it pours. That saying is so true because one morning when I woke up to get myself and the kids ready for school, I looked out my bedroom window to see what the weather was like and noticed that the truck the courts had awarded me was gone.

Yes, the vehicle was gone. At first I thought my ex-husband had come overnight to take back his truck, or he had a family member break into the vehicle to hot wire and steal it. I don't remember how word got to him or how I was able to question him about the vehicle being taken overnight, but I remember my ex-husband saying that he had stopped making payments on the truck. According to him, the truck company had someone repossess it.

I could not believe my ears. I could not believe that a man would stop making payments on a vehicle that any mother who has young children would need.

One thing I know is that no matter what I am going through or where I am in life, I somehow always keep receipts and important documents. Therefore, I was able to telephone the truck company and inquire about the vehicle. I was informed that due to three months of nonpayment, the finance company had the vehicle repossessed.

My first thought was what am I going to do? How am I going to be able to get to class? Will I have to drop out of school? How will I get my baby to day care? I wasn't too concerned for my son because the school bus could pick him up.

Then I began to wonder how this finance company knew that I was awarded possession of my ex-husband's truck, or even where I resided. That was beyond me; I had no idea. Nevertheless, they took possession of the vehicle, and now I was on foot, walking to and from school.

As I mentioned earlier, I contracted pneumonia one winter. Once again, it was no one but God who took care of my children and me, even during this time. It was a local multicultural and nondenominational church that came to our rescue.

The church members and the pastor were phenomenal. I don't remember the name of this church, but I do remember how well my children and I were treated and how genuine their help and love was.

For in the time of trouble he shall hide me in his pavilion: in the secret of his tabernacle shall he hide me; he shall set me up upon a rock. And now shall mine head be lifted up above mine enemies round about me: therefore will I offer in his tabernacle sacrifices of joy; I will sing, yea, I will sing praises unto the Lord (Psalm 27:5–6).

As weeks went on, I was informed about this church's day care and that they would even provide transportation to and from the school for those who did not have reliable transportation. Since I did not have transportation of my own, their services were perfect and right on time. My children even enjoyed the staff, and the staff's energy was always positive and pleasant toward my children.

When I was ill with pneumonia, the members and staff of this church picked up my son, then five years old, and transported him to school. Thereafter, they would pick him up from school and transport him back to the church's after-school day care. As for my daughter, because she was only a year and a half, they would pick her up and keep her all day at the day care, feeding her breakfast, a snack, lunch, another snack, and dinner before bringing her home.

God is our refuge and strength, a very present help in trouble. Therefore will not we fear, though the earth be removed, and though the mountains be carried into the midst of the sea (Psalm 46:1–2).

Even though my son only spent late afternoons at the church day care, he was helped with his homework and provided a snack and dinner before they brought him home. So when the children were brought home, the only thing I had to do was get them ready for their bath and bed. It was so thoughtful of them to help me at this level. I even had help at home.

My son was so helpful too. Not many single moms can say that their five-year-old son grew up overnight to be the man of the home (metaphorically speaking). Yes, while I was ill with pneumonia, my five–year-old baby boy would help me by preparing his little sister's bathwater. He even knew how to check the temperature of the water with his elbow, making certain that it was not too hot for his baby sister.

Once the bathwater was drawn, my son would let me know so I could get up and bathe my daughter. While bathing her, my son would begin coordinating, ironing, and laying out his and his sister's school clothes for the next day. He even repacked her day care bag, making certain she had at least one change of clothes.

Although I was a single mom, I was a single blessed mom.

Train up a child in the way he should go: and when he is old, he will not depart from it (Proverbs 22:6).

Being a single mother was not easy, and I never planned to become a single mother. Then again, who actually does plan to be a single mother? Surely not me. I'm certain there are many strong-willed, career-driven, and financially stable women who believe they don't need help or a husband to raise their child(ren). God bless my sisters.

I believe that, as women, we were designed with a special gift. That gift is to nurture, and although I may not agree with other women who prefer to raise a child without the father involved, that is her prerogative. I am not one to judge people for the decisions they make concerning their lives. I can only speak for myself in that, under better circumstances, I choose to be married, and I prefer that the father of my children be active in their lives.

Look, I'm not here to judge any woman. Whatever works best for other women, I'm happy for them, but during this time, I preferred to be married and raise my children with **a** husband.

And God blessed them, and God said unto them, Be fruitful, and multiply, and replenish the earth, and subdue it: and have dominion over the fish of the sea, and over the fowl of the air, and over every living thing that moveth upon the earth (Genesis 1:28).

I know one thing for certain, and that is I never wanted to become society's statistic, meaning I never wanted my children or me to be labeled or predestined to fail in life. Therefore, removing my children from an unhealthy, abusive environment was something I had to do in order to prevent the cycle from repeating in the next generation.

As a parent, it was my responsibility to protect my children, especially during their most important developmental, innocent, and impressionable years.

As I shared in my first book, *Scarred, but not Broken*, I later was introduced to government assistance. Back in the day and during the 1970s, it was called "welfare." Later, in the '80s, it was called "public or government assistance." Since the '90s, it's been called "TANF, Temporary Assistance for Needed Families."

According to *Indicators of Welfare Dependence: Annual Report to Congress, 2004,* Aid to Families with Dependent Children (AFDC) was established by the Social Security Act of 1935 as a grant program to enable states to provide cash welfare payments for needy children who had been deprived of parental support or care because their father or mother was absent from the home, incapacitated, deceased, or unemployed. All fifty states, the District of Columbia, Guam, Puerto Rico, and the Virgin Islands operated an AFDC program.

When I was growing up and living in the Van Dyke Project in Brooklyn, New York, it was normal to see people exchange food stamps for the purchase of food. As a child, I never really saw the difference because the food stamps were used in the same way as the US dollar.

More or less, I never thought I would be in a position to need government financial assistance. I was reluctant to do so solely because of pride. Oftentimes, when I went grocery shopping, I would witness someone paying for his or her groceries with food stamps, and I would hear other customers in line be so mean and judgmental as they criticized that person. Whether the shopper was Caucasian, Puerto Rican, or African American, the nationality of the individual never mattered; they were always judged and talked about in a negative light by those who were employed or financially stable.

And to think we still have families today receiving some form of government financial assistance due to the job market or unexpected circumstances—and that includes *all* nationalities. There isn't any nationality or group that is exempt from asking for or receiving government financial assistance.

According to the US Bureau of Labor Statistics (Source: *Beyond the Numbers: Prices & Spending*. Vol. 2, No. 26, December 2013.)

Table 1. Characteristics of families with children under 18, by receipt of government means-tested assistance, 2011	
Race (reference person):	
Black or African-American	27.6
White, Asian, and all other races	72.5
Hispanic or Latino origin (reference person):	
Hispanic or Latino	28.8
Not Hispanic or Latino	71.2
(Source: US Bureau of Labor Statistics, Consumer Expenditure Interview Survey.)	

I have no shame to share that I used to receive financial government assistance. If I had allowed my pride to take over, my children and I would have starved to death, or Children and Welfare Services would have intervened and removed my children from my custody on grounds of neglect. Interestingly, the African American family and population have oftentimes been in the forefront as the leading ethnic group to receive government financial assistance, which has caused society to judge this group and believe that these families are the only families receiving assistance. Of course, this has been exaggerated and incorrect throughout time.

Judge not, that ye be not judged. For with what judgment ye judge, ye shall be judged: and with what measure ye mete, it shall be measured to you again. And why beholdest thou the mote that is in thy bother's eye, but considerest not the beam that is in thine own eye? Or how wilt thou say to thy brother, Let me pull out the mote out of thine eye; and behold, a beam is in thine own eye? Thou hypocrite, first cast out the beam out of thine own eye; and then

shalt thou see clearly to cast out the mote out of thy brother's eye (Matthew 7:1–5).

I believe that if I were to do a little more research on statistical data as far back as 1966, when I was born, I'm certain I would discover the data regarding families and populations receiving government financial assistance would be astounding. However, for the purpose of this book, it is irrelevant. I merely wanted to shed some light on my experience receiving government financial assistance and the many individuals who turn up their noses at those who have to resort to this measure of survival as a way to feed their families.

Receiving government financial assistance helped me feed my children, considering that I was not receiving any financial help from their father. Although I was not concerned for me, I was most concerned for their welfare. I never wanted them to go without any food, and they never did, even if it meant that I went without. As a mother, I was okay with going without because I knew my prayers were being heard.

And Jesus said unto them, I am the bread of life; he that cometh to me shall never hunger; and he that believeth on me shall never thirst (John 6:35).

On the contrary, due to life circumstances there are still various nationalities that receive some form of government financial assistance.

As time progressed, I somehow purchased a used vehicle. Yes, I was able to save up $500 from family and friends sending me money for my birthday or extra money to help support the children. I was able to purchase a used 1975 brown Buick. It wasn't much, but it was my vehicle and it got the children and me to and from school and other places we needed to go.

Although I now felt self-sufficient, I was still worried about the actions of my ex-husband. It appeared that no matter where I went or where

I moved to in Illinois, my ex-husband and/or his family learned of my whereabouts. I thought that receiving help from the local church and other God-sent angels who were aligned with me and my children, would make leaving my husband and moving on an easy transition.

Instead, transitioning to freedom from my ex-husband was challenging, to say the least.

It was now almost two years since I had been physically separated from my ex-husband, but he would show up and hide in the college campus parking lot and watch my every action. Yes, it was very creepy because I never knew what he was going to do from one point to the next. I was now going through the last phase of the domestic violence cycle:

- **Phase Four:** Our physical separation, and the flowers and notes left on my car. This phase is known as the **Calm** phase because during this phase things are calm, and the abuser gives gifts. This also can be the most dangerous phase because it is during this

phase that many victims and their child or children are killed.

This phase, in my opinion, is like the calm before the storm.

I discovered that my ex-husband had been stalking me because often there were notes and flowers left on the hood of my car. And although he had come on campus grounds, security had no grounds to have him arrested. According to campus police, because no one was harmed and no crime had been committed, they had no legal ramifications to remove him from campus.

However, during my domestic violence ordeal, I had shared a photo of my ex-husband with the security staff, classmates, and college professors I trusted in case anything ever happened or my ex-husband came on campus looking for me. It was very important that the college campus staff be kept in the loop about what was going on. I wouldn't have been able to live with myself if something tragic happened on campus and some innocent bystander got caught in any crossfire.

One day a male classmate walked me to my vehicle, and there, lying under my wiper blades, was a red rose with a note from my ex-husband telling me that he loved me. There was more written on this note, but this happened over thirty years ago and I don't want to speculate what I "think" it said. I'd rather share and write what is factual and true to the best of my knowledge.

Thereafter, each time I left school I found notes on my vehicle. He then would follow me home and knock on my door. Quite a few times I ignored the knocks and locked the children and me in one of the bedrooms.

While locked in the bedroom, I had in my possession a butcher knife. And because my children had already observed their father's anger, they too were very scared and asked, "Is Daddy going to hurt us?"

Many times I would assure them, "No, Daddy is not going to hurt us." Little did their hearts know that I was willing at that moment to die or go to prison for them if their father broke his way into my home and into that bedroom. Thank God, it usually resulted in a peaceful night.

The Lord is my light and my salvation; whom shall I fear? The Lord is the strength of my life; of whom shall I be afraid? (Psalm 27:1).

As time passed, I decided to return to Texas so I could be closer to family and where I believed that my children and I would be safe. It may have been during the summer when I had a phone conversation with the same aunt who I had visited once upon a time when she and the family were stationed in Norfolk, Virginia.

I shared the specifics with my aunt—that I wanted to start anew and provide a better life for my children and me. But in doing so, I wanted to relocate to a state where I knew my ex-husband would not go.

Therefore, my aunt and uncle, who were on the maternal side of the family, invited me to stay with them. They had relocated to Fort Bragg, North Carolina. While staying with my aunt and uncle, my children remained in Texas with my parents until I could get established with housing and employment and send for them.

During my stay, I was able to obtain employment, and be assigned to a reserve unit in Fort Bragg. My future was beginning to look promising. I began to believe I had a purpose once again.

I later went back to Texas to relocate my children to Fayetteville, North Carolina. I was able to find residency in the Spring Lake area, close to my new reserve unit and not too far from my aunt and uncle. During this transition, I met people from diverse backgrounds at my reserve unit, as well as my neighbors and my coworkers. I no longer had the used Buick. I now was driving a used 1985 Honda Accord.

Believe it or not, I thought I had arrived.

I had my own place and a decent job, I was assigned to a good reserve unit (Quartermaster), I had reliable transportation, and my children were healthy and safe, but there was something that was not right. My spirit was uneasy, and I continued to look sad and disconnected from the people who I came in contact with. I had become guarded, very guarded. I didn't trust anyone to get close to me, or me to them.

I especially did not trust any males, let alone wanted any of them to talk to me. Heck, I didn't even want any of them to look in my direction. Yes, my abusive experience had caused me to become a woman scorned. I began to believe that all men had a hidden agenda and couldn't be truthful about who they were or what they were about.

I had not dated anyone since my divorce, nor did I want to or have any desire to do so. If anything, my focus was on my children and me. However, I ended up connecting with a female sergeant. She and I had a lot in common. For starters, we both were from Brooklyn. I felt safe to be in the company of someone who grew up in the same city, state, and neighborhood as I had. We were able to share similar stories and reminisce about the good times we had growing up in Brooklyn, the diverse New York foods, culture, Broadway shows, and shopping malls.

It all was fun while it lasted, but being in a good place and a safe place did not last long. Little did I know that I had "Abuse Me" written across my forehead.

⌒⌒ ⌒⌒

Lenore E. Walker, a social theorist, was known for her work in 1979 on the social cycle theory of the implementation involving the phases of domestic violence **cycle of abuse** phases. A good illustration of what this cycle looks like is shown below:

Cycle of Abuse

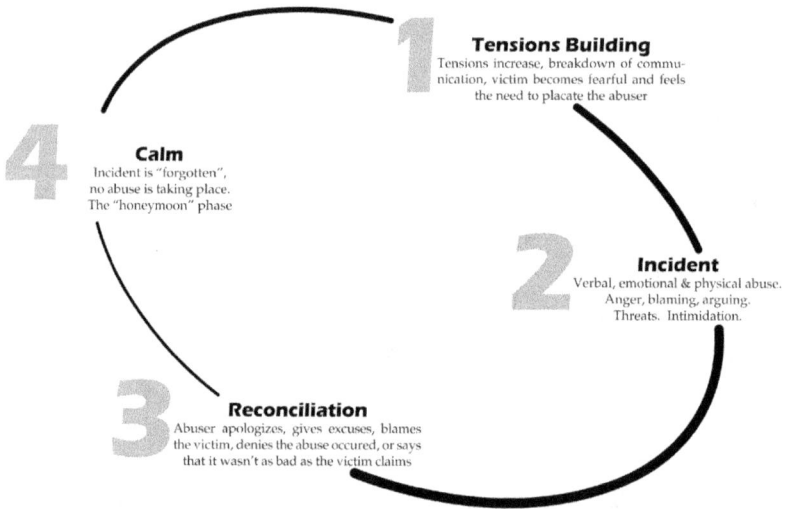

1 Tensions Building
Tensions increase, breakdown of communication, victim becomes fearful and feels the need to placate the abuser

4 Calm
Incident is "forgotten", no abuse is taking place. The "honeymoon" phase

2 Incident
Verbal, emotional & physical abuse. Anger, blaming, arguing. Threats. Intimidation.

3 Reconciliation
Abuser apologizes, gives excuses, blames the victim, denies the abuse occured, or says that it wasn't as bad as the victim claims

During Walker's development, she mentioned that the cycle of abuse focused on the "controlling patriarchal" behavior of male spouses, who believed it was their duty as husbands to maintain power and control by inflicting physical abuse on their wives. Walker later incorporated other labels to bring awareness to the forefront regarding domestic violence's cycle of abuse through associated terminologies, such as the "battering cycle," the "battered woman syndrome," and the "battered person syndrome."

By mentioning the battering cycle and the battered person syndrome, she brought awareness that there are variance levels and forms of abuse. On the contrary, she shared that "abuse does not always lead to physical abuse," and to a great degree, there are abused men just as there are abused women. (Source: Wikipedia: The Free Encyclopedia.)

⚘

One day a colleague brought a male friend of hers to my home. I believe my children were in school at the time. This male friend appeared well put together; he was tall and slim, with a smooth, dark complexion. He was an active-duty staff sergeant assigned to the pharmacy department.

Yes, he worked at the base hospital pharmacy, filling and dispensing prescription medications. He, too, was divorced, and if I remember correctly, he had one son. I later discovered that his ex-wife would not allow him to see or visit his son, but I never understood why, nor did I ask.

Based on what he had disclosed to me, I felt sorry for him, even though I did not know this man well or whether his story had any truth to it. About six months into our relationship, a lightbulb clicked on after he had moved the kids and me into his home. I began to notice a change in him; he would get easily agitated when I asked him a question. No matter what I asked him, he would get agitated, yell, and talk down at me. I knew something wasn't right, yet I ignored the sign.

Oftentimes I would check myself afterward to see if it was something I said or how I said it that spiraled him into complete agitation. It got to the point, however, that nothing I said or did was good enough.

From the food being too cold, too hot, or not seasoned enough, to the kitchen or the house not being clean enough when he came home from work, to the kids making too much noise while he was watching the news, he simply began to find fault with everything I did or did not do.

In the beginning he was a very private person in the neighborhood. Many knew him, and many also respected him. No one disrespected him or his home. I thought he respected our relationship by not allowing his friends to stay too long at his home, now that the kids and I were living with him. The kids had even begun to take to him and he to them.

But all had changed in what appeared to be a nanosecond. I had no idea I was sleeping with the enemy.

Apparently, I had accidently witnessed him selling prescription medications he brought home from the base pharmacy to some of the people and drug addicts in the neighborhood. Yes, I always saw a container sitting on top of the living room television. Each time someone came knocking at the door, I would see him walk over to this container and take something out to give to the person, and in exchange he or she would give him some money.

Honestly, I wasn't certain if there were actual prescription drugs in this large supplement container. Heck, for all I knew, it could have been crack rocks. To this day, I have no idea because I was too afraid to look. I never asked or tried to look into this container.

For one, although I had moved into this man's home, his home did not feel as though it was my home. I still believed that I was only a guest in his home.

Therefore, I did not make his business, my business, but it didn't take a rocket scientist to put two and two together and know what he was involved in was wrong and, most importantly, illegal.

After a while, his home became a revolving door, from late nights with his friends coming over to play spades, drink, and listen to music, to him selling them what was in that container and smoking marijuana. All this activity would take place after I had fed, bathed, and placed the children in bed. However, I was not used to this type of crowd or activities, so when I tried to pull him to the side to ask if he and his friends could take their activity to one of his friend's home, this would only trigger an angry outburst. "If you don't like it, you and your kids can leave," he'd tell me.

Wow, here we go again.

Once again I found myself in a very compromising position. First, it was too late at night to pack my and my children's suitcase and head back to Texas. Secondly, I did not want to have to share with my family once again that I chose the wrong man for my children and me. So I stayed.

Day in and day out his personality and behavior was changing. He no longer was the well-put-together man with a gentle spirit that I had met. No, he had become an evil, narcissistic, mean-spirited, tyrannical monster, who I did not know.

As a result of his wavering behavior, I experienced many nights of unrest. I never knew from one second to the next what he was thinking or what he was about to do. Therefore, the nights were long and the days were even longer.

The days involved the same activities as the nights, just a different time. There were constant sounds of police sirens chasing someone on foot. Sometimes it was an ambulance transporting an individual to the hospital because of a gunshot or stab wound from a domestic violence dispute.

Most importantly, my unrest came from not knowing what mood this man was going to be in the next morning. One thing I did notice, which broke the camel's back for me as a concerned mother, was his relationship toward my children. I observed closely the difference between the way he spoke to my son and the way he spoke to my daughter. He treated my daughter delicately, like a little princess, but when it came to my son, he was very harsh with him even though my son was only seven years old.

What was so alarming to me was how it bothered him when my son cried. He believed boys should be men and men should not cry, let alone show emotion. According to his thought process, he believed that for a male to show emotion was a sign of weakness. Wow, either this was the reason he was not allowed to be in his son's life, or this is what he was taught as a little boy growing up in Panama.

Whatever the reason was for his belief, it was not my belief, and it wasn't working for me.

The warning signs were evident that I was in another unhealthy relationship with a high probability of turning physically violent. And because I knew this cycle all too well, I began to make plans for a safe escape. Seeing and being around this man, I knew the relationship could abruptly result in my children getting caught in the crossfire and being harmed or killed.

Therefore, after my children were released for spring break, I drove them back to Texas. He believed what I told him. I told him that the children always spent the spring and summer break with their grandparents in

Texas. I explained to him that having the children spend time with their grandparents allowed me to work extra hours so I would have extra money to buy them what they needed. Then I usually drove down to get them to resume school.

He accepted my explanation with no problem. I thought, okay, I'm in the clear. Now I just needed to continue my daily routine and not lead him to finding out what my plan of escape was.

And that's exactly what I did. I continued to carry out my daily activities with work, as well as the chores around the house, while the children were gone. I didn't want him to catch on that I was planning to leave him, but somehow he discovered that I was packing and going to leave without notifying him. To this day, I believe he never trusted me and always had someone watching the house while he was at work because he never came home before noon for lunch.

This became a bloody morning. I waited until he left for work, and soon after he left, I rushed and began throwing everything that belonged to the children and me into my vehicle. I didn't care about packing anything neatly. I just wanted out, and I wanted to leave before he came home for lunch at noon.

I remember telephoning my parents a few days earlier to tell them that I was leaving him. My parents told me to be safe. It was no surprise to them because when I noticed his behavior changing over time that is when I began sharing the incidents with my parents. I recall a time when my mother had telephoned to speak to me, and he had told my mother I was not at home.

When she called back and I answered the phone, she mentioned that she'd called earlier but was told that I was out. I shrugged it off and quickly changed the subject since he was listening to our phone conversation.

When I finished my phone conversation with my mother, I asked him if he had answered the phone when my mother called. He said no. I continued to shrug it off and said, "Hmm, maybe she accidently dialed the wrong number." His response was "Yeah, maybe."

All of a sudden and out of nowhere, he quickly turned it around and got on the defensive, trying to pit me against my mother by saying, "You're going to believe your mother over me? I have no reason to lie and say she didn't call, if she didn't call." I said, "Okay, you said she didn't call, and I said she may have dialed a wrong number. That is possible, right?" He didn't say anything after that, and neither did I; I didn't want any trouble.

The time had arrived for me to make a break for it, to leave and never return, so I thought. Apparently, he had other plans and was one step ahead of me.

As I mentioned earlier, I believe he had someone watching the house because he returned home at exactly 10:00 a.m., and my heart dropped. My heart began skipping beats. My heart was racing so fast and so loud that I actually heard it beating.

I had to think fast. He rushed into the room and asked, "What are you doing? Where are you going?" His questions weren't in the tone that you use when you ask someone a question because you simply are clueless and genuinely don't know something. No, his questioning was that of an interrogation.

Yes, his interrogation was that of someone who had been provided with intel, and as a result, he was outraged that I had the audacity to pack up and leave without letting him know.

So I quickly responded with a nonchalant tone and a smile. "Hi, I wasn't expecting you home." I went on to give him this bogus story that "my parents telephoned and asked if I could drive down for the

Memorial Day holiday, and since I miss the children and we don't have any plans for the holiday, I thought I'd just drive down to Texas to spend the holiday with my family."

I continued with my bogus story, including an explanation that "besides, this way I can kill two birds with one stone and bring the children back, so I won't have to drive back to get them when school starts."

Huh, he wasn't buying my story. Yes, I had said a mouthful, but he was not buying it. Somehow he knew I was lying, and his response was "Huh," followed by a right-handed sucker punch to my right eye. I was shocked. I couldn't believe this man had just punched me in my eye.

When I looked up at him, because I was shocked that he hit me, he swung at me and punched me in my eye again. I bent over, and while I was trying to protect my face by covering it, it seemed as though his punches were all deliberately aimed for my face. I caught multiple blows to my back, my head, and my sides too, but I was most concerned about the damage he was trying to do to my face.

Yes, I knew exactly what he was trying to do. This man was trying his best to disfigure my face as a repercussion measure for me trying to leave him.

I guess that by disfiguring my face, he wouldn't have to worry about any man finding me attractive. Based on my personal experience, my undergraduate and graduate studies, as well as my experience having worked at local domestic violence shelters, many perpetrators believed that **"if I can't have you, no one can."**

Although my perpetrator did not express this while he was beating me, it was evident that this was his goal.

However, I was not going to let him succeed. During the entire time he was punching me, I remember praying in my head and calling out to the Lord: "Lord, help me. Don't let this man kill me. Stop him from hitting me; I can't take any more of his punches." All of a sudden, he stopped and stormed outside. I was not certain what he was going outside for or if he was going to return to finish me off or, worse yet, put a bullet in my head.

Though I walk in the midst of trouble, thou wilt revive me: thou shalt stretch forth thine hand against the wrath of mine enemies, and they right hand shall save me (Psalm 138:7).

There I stood with blood drooling from my lip, the entire right side of my face swollen, and my right eye blackened from the blows of his punches. I quickly finished throwing whatever I could in a plastic bag and watched him from the window, pacing back and forth around my car and yelling, "You better go before I kill you."

God is our refuge and strength, a very present help in trouble (Psalm 46:1).

At the first opportunity, I ran to the driver's side to get in my car. I found myself cringe because he raised his fist to hit me again, but he suddenly withheld and walked away while raging, "You better go before I kill you!" I quickly jumped in my car and burned rubber, heading south for Texas.

For I the Lord thy God will hold thy right hand saying unto thee, Fear not; I will help thee (Isaiah 41:13).

Before I left town, I made a stop at my reserve unit to inform them of what transpired. It was evident that some form of a physical altercation had taken place by the blood on my clothes and my swollen face and barely open eye. Ironically, some things your mind just won't let you forget. I remember the weather being warm but breezy. I also remember exactly what I wore on that day. It was a two-piece, cream-colored, pinstriped summer pants set; the vest was sleeveless, and I wore a short-sleeve white blouse with it and a pair of white, flat, open-toe sandals.

It was a Friday, and as I pulled into the reserve center's parking lot, I noticed a few soldiers working in the motor pool. I heard my name called out: "Hey, Sergeant Jones!" I pretended I did not hear them or my name being called; instead I quickly headed to the unit administrator's office. I had a good relationship with my unit administrator, as well as some of the AGRs (Active Guard Reservist), so it was easy to share with her what had just happened.

When I walked in and they saw my condition, they immediately wanted to call the police, as well as notify my abuser's commander since he was active duty.

But I said no. I didn't want any more trouble, and I didn't want to be subpoenaed to return to testify against him. I just wanted out, and I wanted to get as far away from him as I possibly could.

My unit administrator immediately put in an emergency transfer for me to a reserve unit in Grand Prairie, Texas, since that was the city where my parents resided and that was where I was headed for safety. Final hugs were exchanged, tears were shed, and I burned rubber and headed south.

When I pulled into my parents' driveway, I did not take any time to unload the vehicle. Instead I immediately ran to ring the doorbell. The first safe face I saw was my stepfather. I cried, and he didn't ask any questions, so I didn't feel judged. Instead, I remember him saying, "You're home and in a safe place."

My parents had been expecting me, for I had been staying in contact with them the entire time I was living with this man. Yes, he didn't like the fact that I had a strong and tight relationship with my family, especially with my mother. That should have been a sign to leave, but I didn't.

During the time I stayed with my parents, this man called day in and day out. He was able to look through old telephone bills and locate my parents' telephone number. It was like clockwork. He begged me to return to him, and each time I asked him not to call me or my parents' home. After a while his calls began to subside when he realized that I would not be returning.

But of course he had to try one more trick. This time he put a little spin on it by crying on the phone and saying, "If you don't come back to me, I'm going to kill myself; I can't live without you." My last response to him was "go right ahead, and do me and society a favor." I then hung up.

I no longer had sleepless nights; I was at peace and for once I felt safe.

When thou liest down, thou shalt not be afraid: yea, thou shalt lie down, and thy sleep shalt be sweet (Proverbs 3:24).

As I briefly shared in my first book, there are many women and children who are not fortunate enough to be able to remove themselves from a violent environment and as a result are killed by their abuser. For some women, the plan to leave doesn't always pan out as expected, which makes the chance of escaping even more dangerous.

And although there are many more emergency resources that provide services to women and their children who are subjected to domestic violence—more now than ever before—support and awareness for domestic violence will always be needed. Domestic violence is a delicate issue and is more prevalent than ever before.

We hear it and see it more and more on the news every day. It's evident that domestic violence does not discriminate because recently there have been more professional athletes and individuals in the entertainment business, as well as high school and college students, resorting to volatile behaviors with their spouses, partners, and/or significant others.

Consequently, the abused individuals are no different from me or any other woman or man being subjected to domestic violence. Correction, the only difference is economic status.

Yes, these individuals make millions and live in beautiful, lavish mansions, and have ten, fifteen, maybe even twenty vehicles, yet many of them have issues. Many even have unresolved childhood issues that have spilled over into their adult lives. As a result, and because many of them have never owned up to their "stuff" or sought psychiatric help for their unresolved issues, they tend to remain in the social media.

As my title states, domestic violence does not discriminate. Domestic violence affects us all in some shape, form, or fashion. And for every woman who is being abused, it affects her child(ren)'s psychology and their development. For every woman who is killed by her abuser, it still affects her children, family, and friends, and coworkers, who had some relationship or association with that woman.

Nineteen ninety-four was the **last time I allowed a man to physically abuse me!**

O Give thanks unto the Lord, for he is good: for his mercy endureth forever. Let the redeemed of the Lord say so, whom he hath redeemed from the hand of the enemy (Psalm 107:1–2).

2

Verbal Abuse

Verbal abuse is the excessive use of language to undermine someone's dignity and security through insults or humiliation, in a sudden or repeated manner.

—Wikipedia: The Free Encyclopedia, 2015

To think that I was able to remove my children and myself from the unhealthy environment of physical abuse, only to find that I now was subjected to verbal abuse—yes, another form of abuse—but this time it was from my second husband.

I met my second husband while attached to the reserve unit at Fort Bragg. When he learned of my transfer to Texas, he somehow was able to obtain my parents' telephone number. He called me periodically in order to stay in touch and check on how the children and I were doing. He appeared concerned, and once again I allowed my vulnerability to be shown.

He said the right things that I wanted to hear, and before I knew it, we had established a long-distance relationship. He would telephone me every evening, or sometimes every other evening, whenever he did not have to spend long hours at work. He too was prior service and had a very lucrative job; however, he was a reservist, serving one weekend a month.

Once again I was dating a prior service man, who now was serving as a reservist, attached to a reserve unit.

The more we corresponded long distance on the phone, the more we enjoyed talking and getting to know one another. During one of our conversations, he shared that he had never been married. Although he had never been married, he had a three-year-old daughter, who was soon to turn four. By his report, he shared weekend visitation with his daughter's mother. Hearing him speak so highly of his daughter and how active he was in his daughter's life made me admire him even more.

His relationship with his daughter was very special and real. It's sad that children are not able to pick and choose their parents; neither are they to blame for the parents they are given.

But I can truly say that my (second) husband was the epitome of what a true father should exemplify. His daughter never needed nor ever went without anything, which resulted in him often being taken advantage of by his baby's mama, followed by constant day-in and day-out baby mama drama.

Too often society wants to paint the picture that *all* African American men are deadbeat dads, who are not stepping up to take care of their child(ren), when in actuality there are many who do. Unfortunately, those who do are often put under the same scrutiny as those who don't. For the record, just as domestic violence does not discriminate, neither does being a deadbeat father. There are just as many deadbeat fathers in the Caucasian, Hispanic/Latino, and other ethnic populations as there are among African Americans.

Well, the more I found myself admiring his position as a responsible and loving father, the more I allowed myself to let down my guard, and I accepted his invitation for my children and me to visit and meet his family during the Thanksgiving holiday. I was nervous but excited to have an opportunity to meet this man's family. I was always told that if a man introduces you to members in his family, that man has thought about spending the rest of his life with you.

Wow, I thought.

It was now November, and the time to visit his parents and family had arrived. As he started to introduce his parents and his brother, I noticed a little girl present. This little girl was his daughter. I said hello, and like any child that age, she hid her face against her grandmother as though she was shy.

What threw a wrench in the equation was when this little girl told her grandfather to "shut up" and they all laughed, except me. I didn't find it funny that a child was allowed to be disrespectful, especially toward her grandparent. This behavior blew my mind. It was something I was not used to. This was another sign that I ignored.

Another thing I noticed was his relationship with his parents, especially his mother. His father appeared matter of fact, whereas his mother was a spiritual woman. The home was very warm, and the hospitality provided by his mother was well received. I felt at home.

As I write this book, it is becoming more and more evident that I had always received the signs. The signs were always present, telling me to move on and not get involved with the men whom I had chosen to be in the lives of my children and me. But of course, I never listened or took heed to what the signs were telling me.

Now that I look back at all the given signs, I can own it. I simply ignored the signs because at the time it was important to want what I wanted when I wanted it, and it didn't matter how I received it or what the consequences would be.

Months went by, and I continued to visit him, flying back and forth to North Carolina from Texas. Quite a few times the children visited with me, and his parents took a liking to them, as did his daughter. Yes, he always paid the airfare and took great care of my children and me when we visited. There was never any doubt in his mind about my children or me because he knew I was a package deal, and in order to accept me he would have to accept my two children as well.

Accepting my children as his own came easy to him. Wherever we went out in public—to restaurants, movies, even to church—people thought he was my children's father because he treated them as his own. We never wanted for anything; he made certain that we received and had any and everything. His concern was that I was happy.

I had shared with him the history of my past marriage and relationship. My life was an open book; I hid nothing from him nor did I leave any room for doubt or speculation. We were able to talk about anything. He had now become my best male friend. I was always able to talk to him and vent without feeling judged or scrutinized. He never tried to control me or my thoughts. No, I was allowed to be me. I was happy, considering what I had been subjected to in my prior relationship and marriage.

Yes, he wanted to care for me and protect me from any harm. It was almost as if he was my knight in shining armor coming to the aid of a damsel in distress (me).

I soon found myself accepting his hand in marriage. I was elated. Everyone, including both of our families, was excited and happy; even my children were excited and happy. My son, age ten, walked me down the aisle and gave me away, and both of our daughters were flower girls. My wedding was fairly large considering it was held in a suburban North Carolina area.

Everything was exactly how I wanted it, except for one major problem.

This is where I had received another sign that clearly I ignored. Yes, although a bride should be the one to make decisions as to the direction of her wedding, I did not.

Instead, my mother-in-law, the sweet, humble, and spiritual woman, had done a complete 180. I clearly did not know who this woman was. She controlled the entire direction of our wedding, from the music to the food.

For example, my soon-to-be husband and I planned to have a certain R&B song played as I made my entrance and walked down the aisle to the front of the church to join him. However, that did not happen. My soon-to-be mother-in-law had other plans.

Somehow she intervened and asked a senior member of her church to play the organ. So, while standing at the back of the church before my entrance, I was thinking that I was going to hear at least what was heard at other weddings: the "Wedding March"…you know, da dut da da, da dut da da. No, not even that. Instead it sounded like a funeral tune. For a minute I thought I was burying a husband instead of gaining a husband.

Then again, that could had been another sign that my marriage was already dead or destined to die before given a chance.

Yes, I thought I was attending a funeral, as opposed to my own wedding, and I was furious. I would have crawled into a coffin had one been available. But what could I do at that moment? Boy, was I furious.

We had also chosen a slow R&B song for our first dance. That didn't happen either. As a matter of fact, there was no ballroom to dance in, let alone a center floor. No, my soon to be mother-in-law had somehow made changes to that too. What the? I wanted to crawl up and hide my face. This was not the dream wedding that my soon-to-be husband and I had planned.

Initially we had hired a wedding coordinator and planner. But because my mother-in-law insisted on saving us money, she begged us to allow her to plan and coordinate our wedding. We disagreed and instead allowed her to work side by side with the wedding planner and coordinator. We had no idea she was going to run over our wedding coordinator and planner, but apparently she did.

It appears that our wedding coordinator and planner was doomed from the beginning, and I was furious.

When the chance presented itself, I asked my new husband, "Why didn't they play our song when I walked down the aisle? Where was the ballroom or at least the center floor for us to take our first dance?" I told him I felt cheated out of the wedding that I had dreamed about. His response was "Mama thought it would be cheaper to hold everything here in the back of the church."

His response fueled me even more. Here I was furious and sad on my wedding day. It felt like a black cloud was again hanging over my head and my life.

We now were married, and our families were blended. Having a blended family was something I had always said I did not want, but now I had one. Having a blended family was against my better judgment, and later it caused a rift in our marriage, the children, and my relationship with his family and close friends.

All along, my family in Texas never knew what was going on or all the things that had happened under my roof.

The first three years of our marriage were terrific. We always had family nights where we would play games and allow the children to pick and cook meals.

It appeared that we had the perfect marriage but without the white picket fence. People in the neighborhood always drove by to admire our home because it was the largest house in the neighborhood, and we were the only family that had a full basketball court in our backyard for my son and his friends.

Oftentimes my (second) husband would play a one-on-one with my son, and my son enjoyed the relationship he had with his stepfather. Seeing their relationship blossom over time was an awesome sight for any mother.

It is true that there is always one house on a block where children congregate, and that house happened to be ours. Often their parents had to call them home because these children never wanted to leave. No, coming to our home was like coming to a playground because there wasn't a toy or game that my children did not have. Besides, whenever my children's friends came over, I always saw fit to feed them lunch, dinner, a snack, or a drink. I was the "cool" mom.

Although many of the children found me to be the cool mom, I always established rules and boundaries whenever the children from the neighborhood came over. They were not allowed to smoke, drink alcohol, use profanity, or fight in my home. If they did, they were asked to leave and were not allowed to return. No, I didn't play. I was an old-school mom with old-school values.

As I watch many modern-day grandparents and parents, I've noticed that many of them don't set boundaries for their children, let alone their teenagers. I don't know how many times I have witnessed a child or teenager talking back, raising their voice, or cursing at their parents.

Wow, if I had behaved like many of these children do today toward my parents while growing up, I would have been picking up my teeth, as would my children. I came from a family where children respected their elders, and that is the same value I instilled in my children. To this date, my adult children are still respectful toward their elders, including me.

Train up a child in the way he should go: and when he is old, he will not depart from it (Proverbs 22:6).

My second ex-husband was a woman's dream because I never had to work if I didn't want to, but I did. However, before I obtained employment, I continued my goal to complete what I had previously started: my undergraduate studies. But this time, instead of pursuing a degree in prelaw, I just wanted to complete my undergraduate studies and obtain employment.

The paternal aunts were more than submissive to their husbands, so they did not enforce or teach empowerment and independence to the younger females in their family. My maternal aunts were the opposite. According to their values and their teachings to the younger female generation, we were taught never to depend solely on any man. Yet in my earlier relationship and marriage, I found myself modeling my paternal family values as opposed to the maternal values.

If I had mirrored my maternal teachings and values, maybe I would not have been subjected to all of the abuse that I encountered. I'll never know since I'm not able to rewind and rewrite the direction my life should have taken.

I also believe that the loss of my biological father at such a young age could have been a contributing factor in my sense of feeling empty and insecure, and my over-dependency on the men I'd chosen.

As I shared in the first chapter, I gained a new perspective on the direction I wanted to go. I no longer wanted to pursue a degree in prelaw. I no longer wanted to prosecute those who were tried as being guilty or to defend those whom I suspected or knew by firsthand knowledge of being guilty. No, I had and still have a conscience and did not want to be the cause of someone getting the death penalty or serving life in prison for a crime they may not have committed.

Although I no longer wanted to pursue a prelaw degree, I still found criminal justice fascinating; therefore, I continued to pursue my degree in criminal justice. I was blessed during my criminal justice studies to have some awesome professors who provided positive guidance. In short, I was able to obtain my associate's degree and graduated with honors. I later completed and received my bachelor's degree, also with high honors, and was placed on the dean's list.

Initially my intent was not to pursue a bachelor's degree for I was very much content with having accomplished my associate's degree. However, when I came home and shared with my husband that there was an accelerated one-year bachelor's degree program, he insisted that I take advantage of it. I remember his exact words: "Go ahead and enroll and get your bachelor's degree. You don't have to work; I make enough to take care of you and the children." So I did.

I continued and graduated one year later with my bachelor's degree in criminal justice.

While I was pursuing my associate's degree, my husband was so supportive and helpful around the house, and with the children. However, soon after I earned my bachelor's degree, his behavior and attitude toward me changed. He was no longer that supportive husband. No, it appeared as though he was beginning to feel intimidated by my advanced education, making statements like "You think you're better than me since you have some college education now?"

What, seriously? I couldn't believe what I was hearing, and I couldn't understand his sudden change in behavior and attitude. He appeared more and more jealous and intimidated by my advanced education and accomplishment. But why?

As I reminisced about my past relationship and marriage, it was revealed to me that all these men either had no advanced education, or very few college credits. Could it be that my thirst for knowledge had caused these men to despise me, to feel intimidated by me, or to feel jealous? Did my advanced education and accomplishments cause them to feel less of a man? Or were their minds playing tricks on them, having them believe that I thought I was better than them? Only they and the Lord will ever know the truth behind their madness.

If my husband's feeling of intimidation regarding my advanced education was not enough, there were the constant interruptions from his mother and the ongoing baby mama drama. I recall an incident in which my husband had become ill with the flu; we were only three months into our marriage, meaning we were still considered newlyweds. This did not stop my mother in law though.

It was evident that she had no regard or respect for our new marriage because every chance that was made available to her she took advantage of. Similar to my first mother-in-law, she always bulldozed her way into our home even when she was not invited. It was merely power and control.

During the period when my husband took ill, he telephoned his mother to tell her. Instead of her allowing me to do my wifely duties, she invited herself to our home without notice and brought her homemade soup to feed my husband, even though I had already made him soup.

According to her, "My baby needs some homemade soup from his mama." I said to myself, "How dare this woman sashay herself into my home, uninvited, and insult the way that I take care of my sick husband."

She was bold and was not going to back down. There were times I thought that he was married to his mama because she continued to want to do everything for him, even wash his clothes. Yes, apparently, while he was single and living as a bachelor, his mama used to help him out by coming by to wash his clothes, clean his home, and even cook his dinner.

She must not have gotten the wifey memo—the one that said her son was now married and had a wife.

This was not the first time this woman had invited herself to our home, and he never tried to put a stop to it. Once again I married a mama's boy. Throughout our marriage, I had no say about what went on in my home because each time we had a disagreement of any kind, his parents, especially his mother, always knew what was going on with us.

For a time, I could not understand how his parents always knew about everything in our home, from when we had disagreements to when we bought new furniture. It didn't take a rocket scientist to figure out that he was always telling them what was going on. Heck, I began to think I married a little boy in a man's body. My goodness, he always ran to them to share our business, and she never held back in providing her opinion.

Isn't it amazing how people, including in-laws, are always so quick to give their opinions as if they are experts in the field, yet many of them have unresolved issues of their own behind their closed doors? This observation was interesting, very interesting.

With regard to his baby mama drama, we could never buy anything new or try to make any renovations to our home because whatever we did and whatever money was spent, his mother would provide this information to my husband's baby mama. As a result of divulging our business, this gave his baby mama reason to drag my husband back and forth to court for more child support.

If my husband received a ten-cent raise, he shared this information with his mother, who in return would run her mouth to the baby mama. Why? I have no idea.

It appeared as though my mother-in-law was playing devil's advocate. One minute she was praising our marriage and saying how happy she was that her son found a good woman. On the flip side, she was going behind her own son's back and giving information about him and our finances to his baby mama, whom his mother had often said that she did not care too much for.

What a flip side of a crooked coin.

All I know is that the dynamics in this family along with the baby mama was simply a hot mess. I asked myself once again, "What did I get myself into now, and why did I marry a man with this much baggage?"

I knew that more drama was going to surface because each time his daughter came to visit every other weekend, our marriage was challenged. The little girl was intelligent and knew how to win over her grandparents' and father's heart. Although she was now only six years old, she was very manipulative.

I recall a time when my husband was working, and my children, his daughter, and I were at home. When I called the children to the table to eat dinner, she said she did not want to eat; instead she wanted a slice of cake and some ice cream. When I told her that she had to eat dinner before she ate any dessert, she got up from the table and threw a temper tantrum, saying, "My mama said I don't have to listen to you." Excuse me?

Lord knows, if she wasn't a child, I would have told her where she and her mama could go, but I couldn't because she was only repeating what she heard her mother say. I had to catch myself because I was about to chastise someone else's child. Instead I let her go without eating until her father arrived home from work.

When my husband arrived home and I shared with him what had transpired, instead of supporting my decision to not give her cake and ice cream until she ate her dinner, he pampered her and told her that she could have the slice of cake, but before she got some ice cream, she had to eat at least half of the food on her plate. When her father left the kitchen, she turned around to smirk and stuck out her tongue at me.

Lord only knows what I wanted to do, but this was not my child, and I had to realize that it was not her fault; she was a product of her environment. If a tree is not planted with good seed, it will sprout a rotten fruit. So I was not going to lift a hand to her, but Lord knows she needed a good, old you-know-what.

For the remainder our marriage, it was a challenge on a daily basis that resulted in the beginning of the name-calling. Yes, he would call me "stupid," and I would respond, "You're stupid." There were other degrading and choice words that we called one another. We had begun to lose total respect for each other. We had actually fallen out of love.

For the last year of our marriage, we even began sleeping in separate rooms. It had gotten to the point that I despised looking at him. I was no longer attracted to him, and I wanted out of the marriage. We were like two roommates just sharing a home. It appeared that I was not just married to him, but I was married to his parents, his friends, and the baby mama. This was something I did not sign up for, and I was not going to tolerate the disrespect.

Heck, there were times I actually thought I was married to an entire village and not just one man.

The arguing was constant. Every day we argued. I was growing further and further apart from him. I began to see the signs, which were once again evident, but this time I was not going to ignore them. As a precaution, I enrolled my children in tae kwon do.

Enrolling my children in tae kwon do gave them structure and discipline, which helped them at home but even more so in school. Most importantly, it would help keep them safe in case their stepfather became physically violent toward them or me.

There was one incident that involved my fourteen-year-old son running to my rescue. It was one day when my (second) husband and I were in our bedroom arguing. It was so loud that it sounded like some blows were being thrown although that wasn't the case. Instead the sound my son heard was my husband banging his fist on the dresser.

As a result, my son came running in the room with a baseball bat. He was trying to protect me. I remember clearly what my husband asked my son: "What are you planning on doing with that? You hit me with that bat, you better kill me, because I will kill you and your mama." Wow, really?

The next day I enrolled in tae kwon do without my husband's knowledge. I had gone by the dojang and explained to my sabanim (instructor) why I wanted to join. I explained to him that I didn't want my husband to know either. But I knew I had to do this to avoid becoming a victim again at the hands of a man.

No, it wasn't going down like my past incidents. This time it was already set in my mind that I was going to be the one who walked away without a scratch, and definitely without any of my blood being shed. No, if there was going to be someone's blood, it definitely was not going to be mine.

On the day of our tae kwon do tournament, which determined the students who would advance to the next level my husband still had no idea that I was one of the students. He thought I was walking toward the back to help my daughter, who was ten years old at the time, with her dobok (uniform). In actuality, I was heading to the dressing room to put on my uniform. Thus, when he saw me walk to get in position, his mouth dropped. He was shocked. I believe he was afraid.

My husband was the center of attention because not only was my sabanim looking at his reaction but so was everyone else. I believe he was afraid because now he was residing under the roof with a wife and two children who would and could protect themselves, and by any means necessary.

The arguments and threats continued while I continued to go to tae kwon do to perfect my forms and techniques. The situation was so severe that he would threaten to remove the battery, alternator, starter, and tires from my car, so I wouldn't be able to get to work in the morning. To say this man was trying so hard to control me was an understatement.

He knew that he couldn't raise his hand against me, so he took other measures by threatening to disconnect the main components of my vehicle. Yes, he had resorted to childish behavior. I would have never believed it if anyone had told me that he would do such a thing or behave in such an immature manner. Then again, I thought I knew him. But did I really know him? Did I even allow myself to get to know him, or did I get caught up in being so concerned about wanting to be married?

I began stepping back and assessing my situation. I had no one to blame. I allowed myself once again to be placed in a compromising position. Now what was I to do to get out of this situation before someone got injured or seriously hurt?

When I would ask him, "Well, if you tamper with my car, how am I supposed to get to work (the kids were taking the bus to and from school)?" His response was "I don't know; you'll figure it out."

Day in and day out he would throw in my face what he had paid into the house and what was his. I had begun to have zero tolerance, and more and more I wanted out of the marriage. I proceeded to file for a divorce.

The arguments had become very serious to the point that he would also tell me, "If you leave me, ain't no man is going to want you because you have two children." Wow, I actually believed that, but although I did, it didn't stop me from filing for divorce. If anything, his hurtful statements only made it that much easier to leave him.

I had been down this road before, so filing was nothing new to me. Time passed and the divorce was finally granted. My son was now fifteen and a first-degree black belt, and my daughter was almost twelve, and she and I were a high red belt in tae kwon do.

Things were looking good, and we had begun to move on and live our lives without my (second) ex-husband.

Because he knew where I worked, it was like déjà vu. Similar to the behavior from my first husband, my (second) ex-husband would show up at my job, saying "I love you; I'm sorry. I'm missing you and the children." I never gave in, for I had learned the hard way from previous incidents to leave your past in the past and make room for new memories for the present and future.

I have no hard feelings about my (second) ex-husband, for he was a good man, and there were many good times shared and spent together. However, similar to my first husband, I believe he just wasn't ready to step up and show some backbone toward his mother or his baby mama, and I didn't want to carry any of his excess baggage.

But this I say, He which soweth sparingly shall reap also sparingly; and he which soweth bountifully shall reap also bountifully (2 Corinthians 9:6).

As I look back on both of my marriages, I can't help but think that there were some in my family who really liked my first husband, opposed to everyone in my family liking my second husband. But all along no one in my family knew what I was encountering day after day in either of my marriages. As I mentioned in the first chapter, my family had no idea that I was in a very volatile marriage.

One of the other reasons I was reluctant to share what was going on in my marriages was because I believed that when two people are married, they become one, and they should be able to settle any dispute between them, without allowing any outside influences from in-laws or friends. Those outside influences should not be allowed to come in and taint the marriage or the vows that were made before God. With regard to my second marriage, the only thing my family knew was that my second husband had a very lucrative job; therefore, they were not worried because they knew he was financially capable of taking care of my children and me.

Little did they know, he often made it a point to throw in my face that if I left him, no man would want a woman with two small children. Yes, he was a sweet gentleman, went to church every Sunday, knew the Lord, and had even professed to be saved. He was polite and respectful when he was in the presence of friends and his or my family. But at the end of the day, when all the accolades were over, he was ruthless and spiteful behind closed doors.

If there be therefore any consolation in Christ, if any comfort of love, if any fellowship of the Spirit, if any bowels and mercies, fulfill ye my joy, that ye be likeminded, having the same love, being of one accord of one mind. Let nothing be done through strife or vainglory; but in lowliness of mind, let each esteem other better than themselves. Look not every man on his own things, but every man also on the things of others (Philippians 2:1–4).

3

Psychological Abuse

Psychological abuse, also referred to as emotional abuse or mental abuse, is a form of abuse characterized by a person subjecting or exposing another to behavior that may result in psychological trauma, including anxiety, chronic depression, or post-traumatic stress disorder.

—Wikipedia: The Free Encyclopedia, 2015

Psychological, emotional, or mental abuse in my experience is the worst form of abuse. Just like the previous forms of abuse, I have also had my share of psychological, emotional, and/or mental abuse. This form of abuse can tear a person's self-esteem to shreds. Slapping, punching, kicking, cussing, choking, insults, rape, and harassment are just a few characteristics of abuse, which also ranges from emotional and physical to verbal and neglect.

Abuse is a very serious problem in our society, and I believe too often our criminal justice system handles these cases without any sense of empathy. Laws protecting the victim need to be more secure; in addition, harsher penalties need to be implemented on the perpetrator, whether it's his or her first or second offense.

Many questions have been asked, such as why a woman stays in a relationship when she's constantly being battered day in and day out. In my defense, and as I briefly shared in the first chapter, I remained in my abusive relationship because of fear, whether it was with my ex-husbands or in dating relationships. I remained because of the fear of being alone and the fear of not being financially able to support my children and myself.

For other victims who remain in their abusive environment, they may do so because of a lack of advanced education, a lack of employment skills, or the lack of knowledge that there is help and resources available to them and their children. Most importantly, many victims fear losing everything, even their children.

Many abused women grasp on to the Lord and their children for strength and inspiration, making it more rewarding when they survive to later share their stories, as well as being an inspiration to others while providing hope of rising above and becoming victorious.

However, it is duly noted that the road to freedom for a prolonged victim of abuse isn't easy but very dangerous.

Unless an individual has walked in the shoes of a victim of abuse, domestic violence will remain truly misunderstood by curious minds.

Escaping domestic violence is a challenge in and of itself. There are many who make an attempt to leave abusive relationships when they begin to see the detrimental effects of the violence on their children. Many have even sought a civil protection order, which is available in most states. This protective order supposedly removes the abuser from the home while a longer-term arrangement is being made.

Oftentimes the protective order does not stop the perpetrators who have no conscience or fear of repercussions from the court system. As a matter of fact, many perpetrators have ignored the protective order and continued to stalk or begin to play mind games with the victim until the victim believes that they (the perpetrators) are within reach. As a result of this belief, the victims begin to fall into a deep depression and become hypervigilant of their surroundings, even to the extent of paranoia.

Yes, the natural defense mechanism is triggered as a protective shield.

It is equally importantly to know that sometimes the effects of domestic violence are difficult to see if the children are not being physically abused. Others continue to endure their own abuse by believing it is more important for the family to stay together and not realizing how the abuse will affect the children later in life when they begin to date, get into relationships, or even interact with others from a social perspective.

Many abused women who leave with their children seek help from various battered women shelters and programs around the country. In addition, the majority of women who seek safe shelter at these facilities bring one or more children with them. The battered women shelters are an important source of support to children who have experienced domestic violence, and many of these programs have special services for children to help them deal with the trauma and to learn nonviolent tactics.

Yes, we may know about women abuse, spousal abuse, child abuse, and even male abuse. But if we are to seriously address either one, we must recognize the links between these forms of domestic violence. While one form of abuse can certainly occur without the other, the tragic reality is that anytime someone is abused by a wife, husband, or lover, the children are also affected in both overt and subtle ways.

Consequently, when a parent is abused, the children see it, hear it, and sense it. When a parent is abused, the children feel confused, stressed, and fearful. When a parent is abused, often the children begin to feel guilty because they are not able to intervene on behalf of the parent who is being abused. If the parent leaves, the children believe that they are responsible for the family breakup.

Most often, sons who witness a parent being abused are more likely to grow up to repeat the dysfunctional cycle that they witnessed in their early, vulnerable, and innocent years. In addition, when a parent is abused, the children may also be subjected to the abuse by the perpetrator (abuser), or they may be neglected while the helpless, abused parent attempts to deal with his or her own trauma.

As educators, mentors and advocates, we must protect children from physical abuse and help them recognize that they are not responsible for the violence in their homes. We must help them find ways to grow past their hurt into healthy adults. We must also help them to avoid the vicious trap of learned patterns by providing them with positive tools for modeling nonviolent methods of conflict resolution. It is of the utmost importance to help them express their feelings in a healthy and respectful way.

As a society, someone must take the stand to stop the hurt and be the catalyst for change by implementing more support and educational awareness regarding domestic violence. After all, domestic violence does not discriminate.

4

Spousal Sexual Abuse

Spousal sexual abuse is defined as a form of domestic violence. When the abuse involves forced sex, it may constitute rape upon the other spouse, depending on the jurisdiction, and may also constitute an assault. Spousal sexual abuse is also defined as marital rape (also known as spousal rape and rape in marriage), which is non-consensual sex.

—Wikipedia: The Free Encyclopedia, 2015

Today spousal rape is no longer condoned; it is an offense that is given very little, if any, respect, although there are many myths that still surround this issue.

Some of the many myths that are often heard regarding spousal or marital rape are:

- What goes on behind closed doors and in one's bedroom is their business.

- Sexual assault by one's spouse or partner is not serious.

Regardless of one's sexual orientation or whom a person marries or gets involved with, "no" means "no" in every language. Too often the abused find themselves in a very compromising position because they believe their spouse, partner, or significant other will leave them if they refuse any sexual interaction.

Sometimes the sexual abuse by the hands of the spouse, partner, or significant other is followed by physical force and even emotional control, resulting in either the abuser physically beating the victim or threatening to cease all financial support. As I stated in a previous chapter, in many countries women are viewed and treated as property, not respected. Instead, many of these women are used for procreating purposes and as concubines, nothing more.

In our country we have given it a name and a label, that of "spousal sexual abuse" and "marital rape." Among all the previously mentioned forms of abuse, this form is very difficult to prove, especially when the couple is living under the same roof and sleeping in the same bed night after night. Consequently, this form of abuse can be used to discredit someone's character, by going to great lengths to lie and accuse the spouse of rape, especially if the individual wants an out from the marriage but also wants continual financial support from the spouse.

Because the individual is not willing to let go and accept the termination of the marriage—because the spouse is no longer interested or has possibly fallen out of love—then the individual may go through the extreme of accusing the spouse of rape, just to be vindictive.

On the other hand, the spouse may be a great manipulator and report to the authorities that the individual's accusations are the result of a mental breakdown due to an illness, medications, or a recent death in the family. By manipulating the system, he removes himself from being arrested for spousal rape.

If I were to take a poll, I'm certain there would be many people, even in our country and in many of our churches, and private discussions among colleagues who don't believe in this form of abuse. On the contrary, many may believe that when individuals marry, their bodies are not their own but belong to the one whom you've chosen to be your husband or wife.

This form of abuse can be a very hot and controversial subject because of the different views regarding spousal sexual abuse or marital rape.

Someone reading this chapter of the book may say, "Heck, my husband (wife, significant other, or partner) always has excuses, such as a headache, too tired, have to get up early for work, have to get the kids ready, have to study, watching the game, watching my show, have to go to the store, yada yada yada." **News flash! "No" still means "no"—not maybe, I'll think about it, or later. No means no!**

Get it! Got it! Good!

Recap

Many women leave abusive relationships when they begin to see the detrimental effects of domestic violence on their children. Many may seek a civil protection order, available in most states, which removes the abuser from the home while a longer term is being implemented. Yet sometimes the effects of domestic violence are difficult to see if the children are not being physically abused themselves. Consequently, some women may endure their own abuse, believing it is more important for the family to stay together, while not realizing how the abuse is affecting the children.

When a battered woman separates from her husband, boyfriend, or significant other, she fears and often risks losing her children if she lacks the funds to support them on her own. Believe it or not, many abusive fathers have sought and been awarded custody of their children after the divorce has been finalized. However, a number of states have passed laws that require judges to consider evidence of spousal abuse in child custody determinations.

Many abused women who leave with their children seek help from different battered women programs around the country. The majority of women who seek safe shelter through these programs bring one or more children with them. Battered women shelters are an important source of support to children who have experienced domestic violence. Often, these programs have special services for children to help them process the trauma and learn nonviolent tactics for resolutions.

We know about women abuse. We even know about child abuse. But if we are to seriously address either one, we must recognize the links between these two forms of domestic violence. While one form of abuse can certainly occur without the other, the tragic reality is that anytime a mother is abused by her husband, boyfriend, or significant other, her children are also affected overtly and in subtle ways as well. When a mother is abused, her children see it and hear it, and they are able to sense it.

During the abuse, the children feel confused, stressed, fearful, powerless, sad, angry, alone, and even guilty that they are not able to protect their mother or that they are the cause of the problem. In addition, if she leaves, they may feel responsible for the family breakup. Children, especially sons, are more likely to grow up to repeat the dysfunctional patterns that they repeatedly witnessed during their growing years.

It is important to know and understand that children who witness their mother being abused will often suffer from physiological symptoms. Some physiological symptoms that children will experience are depression; withdrawal from other people and from participation in activities; substance abuse to numb oneself from hurting, worrying, or difficulty in concentrating; insomnia and the fear of falling asleep; eating disorders; asthma; stomach ulcers; bed-wetting; stealing; high levels of anxiety; headaches; and temper tantrums. There are many more, but these are the frequent signs often noticed in a child who is subjected to an abusive home environment.

Most importantly, when a mother is abused, her children may also be physically abused, or they may be neglected while she attempts to deal with her own demons (traumas).

Slapping, punching, kicking, cussing, insults, rape, and harassment are a few characteristics of abuse, which ranges from emotional (mental and psychological) to neglect. Domestic violence is a serious problem in today's society, more now than ever before. It has become more prevalent, especially involving professional athletes, military families, and high school and college students.

Many questions have been asked regarding why a woman remains in a volatile relationship when she's constantly being battered day in and day out. As previously illustrated throughout this book, one reason that women remain in the abusive relationship with their abuser is because of fear (first)—fear of being alone and fear of not being financially able to support oneself, especially if the individual lacks advanced education beyond a high school diploma or GED or adequate employment skills.

Another reason is fear of losing everything and their children (second). To many women, their children are their strength and inspiration. For those who survive their abuse, they are able to share their stories, experiences, and how they overcame their abuse primarily because of their faith in the Lord and the strength received from their children. I must remind the curious minds that the road to freedom for a prolonged victim of abuse isn't easy but very challenging and dangerous.

As educators, activists, advocates, and mentors, we must protect our children from the cycle of abuse and help them recognize that they are not responsible for the violence in their homes. We must help them find ways to grow past their hurt into healthy adults. By doing this, we are helping them avoid the vicious trap of learned behavioral patterns of domestic abuse. This can be accomplished by teaching children responsibility and accountability for their actions, and by teaching them through modeling and verbally communicating nonviolent methods of positive family conflict resolution.

Unless an individual has walked in the shoes of someone who has been abused, the domestic violence cycle of abuse will remain misunderstood by the majority of today's society.

Signs That You May Be
in a Domestic Violence Relationship

He or she…

- manipulates you, has extreme mood swings.

- is overly jealous of your relationship with friends and family.

- has a quick temper.

- refuses to compromise or negotiate, or has difficulty communicating what he or she wants.

- always has to be right and in control.

- never apologizes even when knowing he or she is wrong.

- has no sense of humor and always responds to everything seriously.

- takes everything personally.

- refuses to accept breaking up.

- pressures you for sex.

- threatens you.

- has a history of assaults.

- has displayed weapons as a scared or threatening tactic.

- has tantrums by breaking and throwing things.

- punches the wall.

- has unrealistic expectations of you.

- never accepts responsibility for his or her actions.

- He telephone you every day and throughout the day wanting to know what you are doing, where are you, and who you are with.

- views the opposite sex as sex objects with no respect.

- hits you (even if it was once) or has thrown things at you.

- listens to your phone calls.

- checks your cell phone, text messages, house phone caller ID, and messages.

- checks your e-mails and Facebook accounts.

- smells your clothing after you've been out for a long period of time.

- tells you what to wear.

- criticizes more than compliments you.

- is not empathetic to your feelings.

- is very disconnected with emotions.

- is always yelling, screaming, and getting upset over trivial matters, such as spilled milk or unwashed dishes.

- does not want you advancing your education and gets upset if you're reading a book.

- tries to keep you from associating with family or close friends.

- tells you what time to be home.

- gets upset if you're seen speaking to the opposite sex, even if it's an innocent "hello" to your neighbor.

- gets upset because you laugh at a joke told by the opposite sex.

- accuses you of flirting just because you say hello to the opposite sex.

Danger! Stop! Do Not Pass Go!

Signs That You Are a Victim
in a Domestic Violence Cycle of Abuse

- Do you find yourself always pleasing him or her and forgetting about yourself

- Are you experiencing daily and ongoing depression?

- Do you cry more than you did when you were not in the relationship with this person?

- Do you repress your feelings and/or anger?

- Do you withhold from advancing your education because he or she disagrees?

- Do you find yourself always seeking his or her approval before you do anything or go anywhere?

- Do you find yourself walking on eggshells whenever he or she comes home?

- Do you find yourself being extra careful in choosing the right words or conversation piece in order to avoid an argument or confrontation?

- Are you always finding excuses for his or her behaviors?

- Have you let yourself go, gained more weight than you should, or lost more weight because of worrying, or are you careless about how you look?

If the majority of your responses are yes rather than no, as a survivor of domestic violence, I would suggest that you step back and reevaluate your relationship with this person. Ask yourself, what is it about you that has drawn this person to you, or you to them? Life is too short to waste it traveling on a dead-end road.

Helpful Tips for Loving and Pampering Me

- Treat myself to a good movie.

- Get a massage once to twice a month.

- Treat myself to a nice dinner at my favorite seafood restaurant.

- Watch one of my favorite funny videos.

- Exercise.

- Listen to motivational tapes.

- Read scriptures from the Bible for affirmations and a daily walk with God.

- Treat myself to something I can afford with cash at least once a month.

- Read motivational and inspirational books/magazines/poems/tapes.

- Take a warm Epsom salt bath with eucalyptus and spearmint or with lavender oil.

- Journal.

- Relax with Alpha-Stim twice a day.

- Practice healthy dieting; limit excess sugar/starch intake.

- Eliminate pork and red meat from diet.

- Eat lots of vegetables, fruits, and nuts.

- Disassociate myself from people/places and things that are toxic.

Who Am I Today?

Knowing what I will and will not tolerate is one of the key components in establishing my healthy boundaries, and prevents me from allowing myself to be subjected to any forms of abuse. During my ordeal, I had allowed my physical and emotional space to be compromised by individuals who either took over and controlled my space or expected me to be someone other than myself. Today, my emotional space allows me to share my own creativity and individuality. I am free to express who I am and what I am without feeling ostracized or stressed or forced to mimic who I am not, or who someone wants me to be.

When I was created by God, he made me unique and with great precision. Although the shape of my eyes, nose, lips, and ears are similar to many of the members in my paternal and maternal families, I am still unique. My personality makes me unique because it is a blueprint of who I am. It's my individuality; it makes me think differently, behave differently, and form my own opinions.

Over the years I have often been asked the million-dollar question by family, colleagues, close friends, and even strangers: "Will you marry again?" Years ago my response was no. As a matter of fact, I had lost all desire to remarry, let alone believe in the unity of marriage. And for a long time, I never wanted to be among other married couples, especially those who appeared to be happy. As for the other few who appeared unhappy and miserable, let's just say seeing them interact negatively toward one another only confirmed that I never wanted to remarry.

I believe there are many people today who do not respect the unity of their marriage, let alone their spouse. Regardless of how long individuals have been married, I believe doors should always be opened and held by the gentleman. I believe the chair should be pulled out for a woman to be seated. I believe compromise, communication, and empathy are very important ingredients for a successful and healthy marriage.

Also, I believe that marriage should never be sixty-forty, seventy-thirty, or eighty-twenty. I believe that in everything couples do, they ought to do it in a way that will not only complement one another but also complement the marriage. I believe that if many marriages took on the "Ruth and Boaz" attitude, there would be fewer divorces, fewer dysfunctional households, and definitely less domestic violence.

To say that all men are dogs, narcissists, controllers, misogynists, or womanizers, or that they can't be trusted would be generalizing that all men are the same when they are not. Metaphorically speaking, I believe that sometimes we have to walk through the fire and be tried and tested in order for our reward to be great.

Therefore, like Ruth, my Boaz is being specially created with qualities made just for me. He will know what I like and what I don't like. He will accept, understand, and love all of me, attitude and all. He will not judge or criticize me, nor will he have any expectations for me. Instead, he will respect my space and allow me to be me. My Boaz will protect, provide, and love me unconditionally. He will put God first, me second, and everything and everyone else will follow. I will not take a backseat to my place as his wife because wherever we are or wherever we go, people will know, respect, and address me as the "Mrs." The same will apply to him; people will address him as my husband.

(Ruth 1-4)]

I pray that in writing this book and sharing my story, it will not only inspire but also *empower* all those who may be experiencing domestic violence but do not know how to make a safe exit. My prayer for you is this:

He that dwelleth in the secret place of the most High shall abide under the shadow of the Almighty. I will say of the Lord, He is my refuge and my fortress: my God; in him will I Trust. Surely he shall deliver thee from the snare of the fowler, and from the noisome pestilence. He shall cover thee with his feathers, and under his wings shalt thou trust: his truth shall be thy shield and buckler. Thou shalt not be afraid for the terror by night; nor for the arrow that flieth by day. Nor for the pestilence that walketh in darkness; nor for the destruction that wasteth at noonday. A thousand shall fall at thy side, and ten thousand at thy right hand; but it shall not come nigh thee (Psalm 91:1–7).

As I close, I would like to share that as a domestic violence survivor, it is pivotal in my daily walk with God to be cognizant of whom I allow in my world by setting limits. It is equally important to not lose me, but to continue to be free to express who I am, without any demands from anyone, because I am blessed and victorious!

www.ingramcontent.com/pod-product-compliance
Lightning Source LLC
LaVergne TN
LVHW051702080426
835511LV00017B/2686